An Institutional Investor Publication

FINANCIAL FUTURES AND OPTIONS

Managing Risk in the Interest Rate, Currency and Equity Markets

Ira G. Kawaller

PROBUS PUBLISHING COMPANY
Chicago, Illinois
Cambridge, England

To Geremy, Ben, and Zoë

Contents

Contents

List of Tables and Figures

List of Tables

List of Figures

List of Tables and Figures

Foreword

For all their seeming complexity, futures and options provide only three things: risk management, price discovery, and asset allocation. They offer investors, portfolio managers, and corporate treasury officers cost-effective mechanisms for dealing with the prospect of an adverse price development, thereby reducing exposure to any particular negative outcome.

If, for example, the Chief Financial Officer of a U.S. multinational faces contractual obligations in deutsche marks, his concern is that the company might fulfill the terms of the contract and still lose money if there is volatility in currency markets. The most cost-effective way of eliminating this risk and "discovering" the future price of the DM is through a futures contract or option, which permits the CFO to take delivery of (or take an option to buy) a given quantity of DM at a fixed rate on a certain day. If the DM goes up on world markets, his hedge generates a compensating gain. But even if the DM drops or stays the same, he also wins. In this case he wins because he insured that the profit margins of his company were not eroded by macroeconomic market forces beyond his control.

What is true of this hypothetical DM exposure is equally true of oil, grain, metals, bonds, stocks or any of the hundreds of items traded on financial and commodity markets worldwide. The need to insure against loss, combined with the internationalization of the economy and the uncertainty it brings, explains why futures and options contracts have been growing in volume and variety.

So rapid has the growth been that the center of gravity for institutional investment is undergoing a shift away from traditional equity exchanges toward futures and options exchanges. As for the future, the direction seems clear: continued growth—by leaps and bounds—anywhere markets are free and liquidity is available. Over the past decade, futures and options trading in the U.S. has expanded by a rate in excess of 300 percent. At the same time, the U.S. share of this business went from a virtual monopoly to approximately half of the world-wide total. Moreover, nearly every major financial center has or is planning a futures and options exchange, with interest shown most recently from such new quarters as Mexico, Panama, Hungary, and the countries of the now-defunct Soviet Union.

Are there no constraints? Of course there are. But the limitations are our own doing. Certainly the regulatory environment can influence the development of this business activity, either beneficially or adversely, depending on the nature of regulations in question. On a more personal level, however, knowledge is the key. The risk manager of today must take the time and commit the resources to learn appropriate hedging techniques. Given that the primary rationale for this activity is to manage uncertainty, today's financial manager must bring to the table the expertise to deliver on the promise of reducing risk.

This requisite expertise doesn't come free, but this book has made it less expensive! With a clear, step-by-step presentation, the book makes a wide range of strategies and tactics more accessible—whether appropriate for managing risks associated with currency fluctuations, interest rate moves, or stock price gyrations. Incorporation of the strategies and tactics described here will undoubtedly help to keep open the doors of opportunity, for tomorrow and beyond.

John F. Sandner*
Chairman, Board of Governors
Chicago Mercantile Exchange

*Mr. Sandner is in his eighth term as chairman of the Board of Governors of CME, the world's largest exchange of financial futures and options. He is widely regarded as having pioneered the development of this marketplace.

Preface

Since joining the Chicago Mercantile Exchange in 1981, my overriding objective as director of the New York office has been to teach market professionals—bankers, brokers, pension managers, currency dealers, and corporate financial officers—how to use futures and options to manage risk and exploit trading opportunities. In the early years, much of my effort went into refining materials that explained the basics of how these instruments work. But as the years went on, I had the opportunity to discover some tricks, nuances, and idiosyncrasies of these instruments that may not be apparent at first glance. This book is an effort to bring to light some of the more esoteric aspects of futures and options, to help users and potential users better understand the capabilities of these instruments, and to diminish the prospect of realizing "surprising" results.

The book is divided into three sections, one each on interest rates, currencies, and stock index futures and options. Each chapter is designed to be largely self-sufficient. A basic knowledge of the markets is presumed, so that little in the way of introductory material is offered. Rather, each chapter deals with the pricing and arbitrage, hedging, or trading applications of the instruments contained therein. A person who trades in one particular market area might very well focus on the portions of a section that coincide most closely with his or her area of interest. In some cases, however, though a chapter treats concepts within the context of a one-market area, the issues covered have more generic ramifications. For example, Chapter Three, "Finding Trading Opportunities with Interest Rate Futures," is written about Eurodollar futures markets, but the ideas presented are likely to be relevant in certain instances for currency (and perhaps other) traders as well. Similarly, Chapter One, "New Tools for Managing Interest Rate Risk," also presents an approach to managing risk that is applicable to other situations.

In all cases, the articles are written with practical considerations in mind: How should these instruments be used, and what can the user expect as a result?

Ira G. Kawaller

Acknowledgments

I am indebted to the Chicago Mercantile Exchange for providing the environment and the encouragement that permitted me to write the articles contained in this book. Of course, it is the people at the Chicago Mercantile Exchange—the staff and the Exchange leadership—that really deserve mention. In particular: Leo Melamed, for having the foresight and authority within the Exchange community to plant the seeds and nurture the growth of what has become a truly unique engine of innovation; William Brodsky, President of the Exchange, and Jack Sandner, the Chairman, for their roles in the administration of the Exchange; Barbara Richards and Larry Geraghty, my current and former superiors in charge of the Marketing Department, who deserve the most direct credit for securing the resources and making education a focal point of the CME's marketing effort; and Fran DeRose, who warrants a special acknowledgment and thanks. Ms. DeRose has been my personal secretary, office manager, and friend for the ten years that I have been at the Chicago Mercantile Exchange. She has typed (and re-typed) every word in this book, using the highest standards of professionalism. Jim Slentz and Leslie Wurman, colleagues in the CME marketing department, also deserve credit for helpful suggestions in connnection with many of the chapters.

Outside the CME, I want to thank Tim Koch and Paul Koch, Professors at the University of South Carolina and the

University of Kansas, respectively, for their contributions as co-authors of a number of articles included in the text and for their helpful comments and direction in many of the other pieces.

Part

I

Interest Rates

Chapter

1

New Tools for Managing Interest Rate Risk

G iven a forecast for markedly different interest rates, managers of financial institutions and corporations may have a decision to make. On the one hand, if the expected rate change is beneficial, no action would be required. But, on the other hand, if the expectation calls for an adverse interest rate move, it certainly would be appropriate to consider a defensive measure.

Hedging with interest rate futures contracts is one way of achieving the desired protection, and this approach is clearly growing in use and gaining increasing acceptance. But recent innovations in financial markets have added yet another tool to the financial managers' arsenal: options on interest rate futures can now be used to manage interest rate risk.

In this chapter, the discussion and examples will focus on Eurodollar futures and options traded at the Chicago Mercantile Exchange.

Eurodollar Futures

The Eurodollar futures contract is a price-fixing mechanism that allows for the setting of the offered rate on a three-month Eurodollar time deposit, commencing on the third Wednesday of

March, June, September, or December, depending on the contract expiration month. Operationally, futures prices are derived by subtracting an interest rate (in percentage points, carried to two decimal places) from 100. Therefore, as interest rates rise, futures prices will fall, and vice versa. Since the face amount of the Eurodollar futures is $1 million and its maturity is three months, every basis-point move in the futures price (yield) translates to a value of $25. In general, movements in the Eurodollar futures market will be closely correlated to yield movements in the underlying Eurodollar time deposit market, even though changes will not be precisely equal over any given period of time.

As long as one maintains the futures position—either long (hoping the market will rise in price, decline in yield) or short (hoping the market will decline in price, rise in yield)—the participant will be obligated to mark the contract to market on a daily basis and settle any change in value daily, in cash. This obligation can be terminated at any time by simply "trading out" of the position (i.e., making the opposite transaction). Upon the expiration of the contract, any participant still maintaining contracts will have a final mark-to-market adjustment, with the final settlement price based on an average derived from a survey of London bankers who report their perception of the cash-market three-month offered rate at the time of the survey.

When using this contract for hedging purposes, the hedger will buy or sell enough futures contracts to provide a dollar-for-dollar offset to an adverse move in interest rates. For example, the funding manager who would suffer under rising interest rates would be a seller of futures contracts. In this case, if rates do rise, the banker will necessarily take in deposits at a higher rate; but the increased cost due to the marginal change in interest rates will be offset by futures profits. Conversely, if rates happen to decline, the lower cost of funds would be offset by futures losses. In some sense, then, the use of futures as a hedging device is a rate-setting mechanism that insulates the hedger from forthcoming interest rate effects—either beneficial or adverse.

Basic Features of Options on Eurodollar Futures

Options come in two types—calls and puts. Calls are the right to buy something at a fixed price. Puts are the right to sell at a fixed price. Both calls and puts have a limited period for which they are in effect. A June call, for example, expires sometime in June; a September put expires in September, and so on. The fixed price is called the exercise or strike price. For example, an 89.00-strike June call on a Eurodollar futures contract gives the buyer of this option the right to purchase a June Eurodollar futures contract at a price of 89.00.[1] The right terminates in June. It should be clear that the right will go unexercised if the underlying futures can be purchased in the open market for *less than* 89.00. In this case, this option is called "out-of-the-money." If the market for June futures is trading at a price greater than 89.00, the 89.00-strike-call option would be called "in-the-money." When the futures price equals the strike price, the option is called "at-the-money."

The following points must be understood in order to use options and futures advantageously:

The exercise of an option on a futures contract results in the establishment of a futures position. Upon exercise, the buyer of a call option will hold a long futures position, initiated at the exercise price, while the seller of that call will be assigned a short futures position, also entered at the strike price. Conversely, the buyer of a put position will establish a short futures position at the strike price upon exercise, while the seller of the put will be assigned a long futures position at the exercise price. In all cases following the establishment of a futures position, the resulting futures contracts will be marked-to-market at the close of the next business day, and from then on until liquidation of the underlying futures position.

The price of the option can be divided between its intrinsic value and its time value. Intrinsic value is the amount that an option is in-the-money, and that is the amount that the underlying instrument is above the strike price for the call or below the strike price for the put. The time value, which is any excess of the option price above its intrinsic value, decays as the expiration of the option approaches.

When holding options to expiration, a call will make money only if the underlying instrument rises above the strike price, plus the price paid for the option. A put will make money only if the underlying security falls below the strike, less the price paid for the option.

Option buyers pay for their option at the time of purchase. No further cash-flow adjustments are required until the option either is exercised or sold. Option sellers, on the other hand, receive the price of the option upon its sale. With exchange-traded options, however, sellers must post a margin deposit with the appropriate exchange (via their broker). This margin amount will typically exceed the price of the option. Moreover, if the option appreciates in value, additional margin is likely to be required.

In general, call option prices move directly with the price of the underlying future contracts, and put option prices move inversely with the price of the underlying future contracts. The relative price movement of the option as compared to the futures contract depends upon the relationship between the underlying futures price and the exercise price of the option. At price extremes, when an option is deep in-the-money, the option will move almost one-for-one with the underlying futures contract. In this case, we say that the delta approaches unity (+1 for calls, –1 for puts). When options are deep out-of-the-money, the relative move of the option with the underlying futures contract (or the delta) approaches zero. For at-the-money options, the delta is about .5. Deltas also will vary with the time to maturity, as well as with price fluctuations.

Uses of Options and Futures

Consider dividing the world between those who would be adversely affected by rising interest rates (prospective borrowers as well as investors holding fixed-income assets) and those who would be adversely affected by declining interest rates (prospective investors in fixed-income assets). In the first case, managers would be interested in identifying some instrument that would generate offsetting profits during periods of rising interest rates. In the second case, managers would look for an instrument that would generate profits during periods of declining interest rates.

These two cases will be considered separately.

Generating Profit with Rising Interest Rates

The manager has three choices for dealing with an expectation of rising interest rates: 1) Selling (or shorting) an interest rate futures contract, 2) buying a put option, or 3) selling a call option. All will make money if interest rates do, in fact, rise. Each alternative will have a different outcome, however, depending upon how interest rates actually change—independent of expectations. For the futures contract, for instance, the opportunities and risks are symmetric. That is, the financial manager could realize virtually unlimited profits with this instrument; but he or she alternatively could realize virtually unlimited losses if interest rates do not move as expected.

Buying the put allows profits to be generated from rising interest rates, but if rates decline, the exposure to loss is limited to the price of that option. Put buying may be seen as analogous to purchasing insurance with a deductible clause. A claim can be filed if interest rates rise, and the insurance policy will pay off. Conversely, if interest rates do not rise, or if they fall, the put buyer simply lives with the fact that he paid for insurance, but does not file a claim.

Finally, the call seller has still another opportunity/risk profile. If interest rates go up as expected, the call will lose value, and thus it can be bought back for less. As a result, the call seller would get to keep some—and perhaps all—of the initial selling price of the option. On the other hand, if interest rates decline, the option price will rise, and the call seller will be forced to buy back his option position at a higher price—therefore at a loss. In other words, by choosing this method of coverage, the manager only achieves profits for a relatively minor interest rate increase, but he or she is completely exposed to a loss if rates unexpectedly decline. These various opportunities/risk differences are summarized in Table 1-1.

Generating Profit with Declining Interest Rates

For those who would suffer under declining interest rates, all the solutions are the opposite of those just presented. That is, the choice now becomes: 1) Buying a futures contract, 2) buying a call option, or 3) selling a put option. The characteristics are analogous: Futures offer symmetric profit opportunity and risk, option buying (calls) offers unbounded profit potential and limited risk, and selling options (puts) offers limited profit potential and unbounded risk. Table 1-2 shows possible outcomes for those desiring to generate profit when interest rates are declining.

Summary and Conclusion

The determination of which hedging strategy is best—that is, whether to use a futures contract, buy an option (a call to pro-

Table 1-1: Profiting from Rising Interest Rates
(Declining Futures Prices)

Futures At Expiration	Sell Futures @ 90.00	Buy 90 Put @ 1.00	Sell 90 Call @ 1.00
93.00	–3.00	–1.00	–2.00
91.00	–1.00	–1.00	Break even
90.00	Break even	–1.00	+1.00
89.00	+1.00	Break even	+1.00
87.00	+3.00	+2.00	+1.00

Table 1-2: Profiting from Declining Interest Rates
(Rising Futures Prices)

Futures At Expiration	Buy Futures @ 90.00	Buy 90 Put @ 1.00	Sell 90 Call @ 1.00
93.00	+3.00	+2.00	+1.00
91.00	+1.00	Break even	+1.00
90.00	Break even	–1.00	+1.00
89.00	–1.00	–1.00	Break even
87.00	–3.00	–1.00	–2.00

tect against declining interest rates or a put to protect against rising interest rates), or sell an option (the opposite of the long option choice)—is unclear at the time the hedge is initiated. In fact, depending on how the underlying interest rate changes, any one of the three choices can be the best. The manager's choice should depend on 1) the certainty that the manager attaches to the associated interest rate forecast and 2) the comfort level associated with the risks among the three choices. Referring to either of the two Tables presented, one can see that the manager who has great confidence in his or her forecast and an expectation of a sizable interest rate move would be best served by a futures contract. Alternatively, if one expected a large move but had a lesser degree of confidence in the forecast, the long option would be preferred. And, finally, the short option choice would be best only when relatively small rate moves are anticipated.

From the perspective of a hedger, the choices and trade-offs can be stated in the following way: Hedging with futures insulates the hedger from the effects of subsequent interest rate moves—either adverse or beneficial. Buying options is analogous to purchasing insurance for one-way protection. Finally, selling options offers a fixed maximum amount of protection and the risk of non protection for major adverse interest rate changes. Therefore, it becomes the manager's responsibility to understand the three choices and the risks and opportunities associated with each.

This chapter is reprinted with permission of Bank Administration Institute from *World of Banking,* July/August 1985.

Endnotes

1   For options expiring on the March quarterly cycle (i.e., March, June, September, and December), the underlying futures have a common expiration; for non-quarterly options the underlying futures is the next quarterly expiration. That is, for the January options, the March futures is the underlying instrument, etc.

Chapter

2

Identifying
Cheap Sources
of Funds

F or those funding managers whose cost of funds closely corre- lates to Eurodollar interest rates (e.g., the London Interbank Offered Rate, LIBOR), failure to consider the use of Eurodol- lar futures contracts could be a costly decision. These instru- ments, traded at the Chicago Mercantile Exchange, can be used either to lengthen or shorten the maturity structure of the bank's liabilities in a synthetic manner, often resulting in cheaper funds than would oth- erwise be the case. This chapter will explain how to evaluate whether Eurodollar futures contracts can, in fact, effectively reduce the cost of funds. Before the criteria are explained, some background is offered on the Eurodollar market and Eurodollar futures contracts.

Eurodollar Deposits

A Eurodollar deposit is simply a dollar-denominated, interest- bearing bank deposit maintained outside the boundaries of the United States. Two types of deposits are available: *certificates of deposit*, which are traded in a secondary market, and *time depos- its*, which are not. In both cases, maturities can vary, but they are typically three, six, and 12 months.

Eurodollar deposits are priced in terms of yield, with bids and offers quoted in sixteenths. The bid side reflects the rate that banks are willing to pay for their deposits. The offered side is the rate that banks are willing to take when placing funds at other institutions in the interbank market.

The LIBOR is somewhat of a benchmark rate for the Eurodollar market. In a sense, it is a fixing in the London market of the offered side of the Eurodollar time deposit market at a specific time each day. It is important for this discussion in that the Eurodollar futures contract settles to the three-month offered rate at the expiration of the contract.

Eurodollar Futures Contracts

Turning to the futures contract, the Eurodollar futures is a market for three-month Eurodollar time deposits, commencing on a specific forthcoming date (the third Wednesday of March, June, September, or December, depending on the contract expiration month[1]). Operationally, futures prices are derived by subtracting an interest rate (in percentage points, carried to two decimal places) from 100. Therefore, as interest rates rise, futures prices will fall, and vice versa. As the face amount of the Eurodollar futures is $1 million and its maturity is three months, every basis point move in the futures price (yield) translates to a value of $25. In general, movements in the Eurodollar futures market will be closely correlated to yield movements in the underlying Eurodollar time deposit market, although changes will not be precisely equal over any given time period.

As long as one maintains the futures position, either long (which would profit from a rise in price, decline in yield) or short (which would profit from a decline in price, rise in yield), the participant will be obligated to mark the contract to market on a daily basis and settle any change in value daily in cash. This obligation can be terminated at any time by simply "trading out" of the position (i.e., making the opposite transaction).

Upon the expiration of the contract, any participant still maintaining contracts will have a final mark-to-market adjustment, with the final settlement price of the futures contract determined by a survey of London bankers who report their perception of the cash market three-month LIBOR at the time of the survey. The final settlement value for the futures contract will be the average rate from the survey deducted from 100. For instance, if the survey results in an average rate of 7 percent, the final futures price will be 93.00.

Identifying Funding Opportunities

For the purpose of this example, assume that the institution can borrow at LIBOR. Suppose a funding manager has been instructed to raise $100 million with three-month Eurodollar deposits and $50 million with a six-month term. The astute manager would want to know whether the best rates are available directly in the Eurodollar deposit market or indirectly, using the Eurodollar futures in combination with cash market instruments. Assume the following conditions hold:

> Quotations on 9/13
> > Three-month LIBOR: 7.00%
> > Six-month LIBOR: 7.37%
> > December futures price: 92.80

Further assume that this institution funds at LIBOR. If, in fact, funding typically was handled at a spread over or under LIBOR, the above rates would have to be adjusted up or down by the appropriate spread.

The construction of the synthetic six-month deposit involves issuing three-month deposits at 7.00 percent on September 15 (i.e., two business days after the trade date) and simultaneously hedging a subsequent reissuance of deposits three months later by selling December futures contracts. On December 13—again, two business days before December 15—the hedge would be lifted, and deposits would be reissued two business days later. Given a December futures price of 92.80 on September 13, the target funding rate for the second three-month period is 7.20 percent (100.00 - 92.80 = 7.20). The expected rate for the full six-month period is found using the standard compounding formula and solving for R_{6mo}:[2]

$$(1 + .0700 \left[\frac{91}{360}\right]) \ (1 + .0720 \left[\frac{91}{360}\right]) = (1 + R_{6mo} \left[\frac{182}{360}\right])$$

In this case, the all-inclusive rate the manager could expect to pay when raising funds this way would be 7.16 percent, as opposed to the rate available by issuing Eurodollar deposits directly at 7.37 percent.

In the case of the three-month deposits, again the manager could simply issue three-month deposits, or he could issue six-month deposits and *buy* futures as an offset for the second half of the period. The resulting three-month rate would be found by solving for R_{3mo} from the following formula:

$$(1 + R_{3mo} \left[\frac{91}{360}\right]) = \frac{(1 + .0737 \left[\frac{182}{360}\right])}{(1 + .0720 \left[\frac{91}{360}\right])}$$

Thus, $R_{3mo} = .0741$ or 7.41 percent, as compared to the straightforward funding rate of 7.00 percent by directly issuing three-month deposits.

With these calculations completed, the funding manager is now in a position to make a decision. Six-month money is cheaper when raised synthetically with three-month deposits and short futures, and three-month money is cheaper when raised directly with a three-month deposit. Given this determination, the remainder of this chapter will deal with the mechanics of raising six-month money synthetically, via the cash/futures combination.

The hedge must now cover the reissuance of deposits on December 15 in an amount equal to the original $50 million plus the interest due after the first three months.[3] In other words, the exposure for December 15 would be the original $50 million, multiplied by $(1 + .0700 \left[\dfrac{91}{360} \right])$ or $50.9 million.[4] As one contract is needed for each $1 million of three-month exposure, the correct hedge would call for selling 51 Eurodollar futures contracts.

The following sequence reflects the steps to be taken and possible results:

1. 9/13   a) Arrange to issue $50 million three-month Eurodollar deposits on 9/15 @ 7.00 percent; and

            b) Sell 51 December ED futures @ 92.80.

2. 12/13   a) Offset (buy) 51 December Eurodollar futures at the market price; and

            b) Arrange to issue $50.9 million three-month deposits, less (or plus) futures profits (or losses) generated over the first three months, on 12/15.

If rates rise between September 13 and December 13, the second deposit issuance will be more costly, but this extra cost will be offset by profits on the 51 Eurodollar futures contracts. On the other hand, if rates fall during that time, the benefit of the lower reissuance will be foregone by futures' losses.

Looking more closely at the seemingly less attractive case when rates decline and the futures position generates losses, suppose the three-month Eurodollar deposit rate on December 13 declined to 5.00 percent and the December Eurodollar futures were trading at 95.00 (5.00 percent). The following figures would apply:

Interest paid on initial three-month deposit:

$$\$50 \text{ million} \times .0700 \times \left(\frac{91}{360}\right) = \$884,720$$

Futures results:

$$51 \times (9280 - 9500) \times \$25 = -\$280,500$$

Amount reissued on December 15 (principal plus interest plus futures losses):

$$50,000,000 + 884,720 + 280,500 = \$51,165,220$$

Interest paid on December 15 deposit issuance:

$$\$51,165,220 \times .05 \times \left(\frac{91}{360}\right) = \$646,672$$

Total interest plus futures losses:

$$884,720 + 646,672 + 280,500 = \$1,811,892$$

Total cost of funds as an annual money market yield:

$$\left(\frac{1,811.892}{50,000,000}\right) \times \left(\frac{360}{182}\right) = .0717 \text{ or } 7.17 \text{ percent}$$

Recalling that original intention of "locking-up" a funding rate of 7.16 percent, the exercise of examining the dollar flows demonstrates the robustness of the hedge projections.[5]

A Major Caveat

In the real world, things do not always line up quite so nicely as in our examples, where the hedge is timed so that the futures contract expires simultaneously with the reissuance of the deposit. Unfortunately, this situation only occurs four times a year. What about the other times? The same evaluation must be made, but one judgmental adjustment is needed to reflect the prospect of non-convergence between futures rate (100 minus the futures price) and the rate on the reissued deposit. Whatever the degree of the non-convergence in terms of basis points, the effect for the six-month term would be one-half the size of the non-convergence basis. For example, a 30-basis-point difference would translate to the 15-basis-point effect on an annual basis, as it is spread over two quarters. Comparing the futures rate to LIBOR at the time of the deposit reissuance, if LIBOR were lower, the cost of funds would be 15 basis points below the original target, while a higher LIBOR could increase our cost of funds to 15 basis points above the original target.

Summary

The above example demonstrates an unambiguous situation where futures contracts improve the performance of the funding manager. Though the example is hypothetical, the availability of such opportunities is very real. Of course, the benefits will accrue only to those who make the necessary comparison of the cost of synthetic funding to those associated with the more typical, straight Eurodollar funding. Ignoring this synthetic strategy, however, dooms the funding manager to paying a premium for funds each and every time that manager accesses the market.

This chapter is reprinted from *Financial Managers' Statement*, January 1981, with the permission of, and copyrighted 1987 by, the Financial Managers Society, Inc., 111 E. Wacker Drive, Chicago, Illinois 60601.

Endnotes

1   Futures trading ends two London business days prior to the third Wednesday.

2   This formula assumes a 91-day maturity for both the initial Eurodollar issuance on September 15 and the reissuance on December 15. In some instances 90 or 92 days might be correct.

3   In fact, futures' gains or losses will also affect this total, as will be shown, but on March 15 the eventual futures' results are uncertain.

4   The figure is rounded to the nearest hundred thousand.

5   The slight difference arises largely because the value of a basis point for the 91-day cash instrument is $25.28, slightly more than the $25-dollar value of a basis point for the futures contract, which assumes a hypothetical 90-day maturity for the underlying instrument.

Chapter

3

Finding Trading Opportunities with Interest Rate Futures

I t is reasonably well recognized by the professional financial community that futures markets offer attractive complements to traditional cash markets. And in large part due to good liquidity, low transactions cost, attractive leverage, and limited credit risk exposure, a growing number of financial managers have implemented the use of futures for risk management purposes. In these hedging applications, the outcome from the futures position will tend to offset price movements in some underlying business exposure already present for the firm. While hedging is often the starting point for professional financial managers, however, most move on to discover attractive trading opportunities as well.

Having the flexibility, authority, and experience with futures contracts often puts the manager in a position to exploit attractive market situations. This chapter focuses on two specific issues. The first deals with the concept of the futures basis—the difference between the futures price and the price of the underlying instrument. The second concerns the availability of mispriced futures, specifically with respect to the Eurodollar and LIBOR contracts. The discussion should sensitize the reader to the availability of potentially rewarding trading opportunities.

Basis Issues

A Few Examples

Suppose you believe short-term interest rates are poised to decline. How could you position yourself in the futures market to make money if your view turns out to be correct? Most would unhesitatingly respond, "buy Eurodollar, LIBOR, or T-bill futures." In fact, that answer might be ill-advised—at least under certain circumstances. Conceivably, one might want to rethink the response if (a) the time frame for the expected rate move were reasonably extended (i.e., over some months); or (b) the basis already incorporated the expected move.

Consider the following example dealing with Eurodollars. With 2½ months to the nearby contracts' expiration, three-month LIBOR on Eurodollar time deposits is trading at 8.75 percent. Suppose further that you expect rates to drop by 50 basis points by the expiration date. Under these circumstances, whether you should buy Eurodollar futures depends on their price. Specifically, a price of 91.75 is a critical value. As long as you buy at a price below 91.75, the trade is consistent with your views; but if the futures are priced higher, you should actually be a willing seller. With LIBOR dropping to 8.25 percent, the futures price will settle at 91.75 (100 minus 8.25). Clearly, if one initially sold at a higher price, the trade would generate a gain.

In the typical case, the basis is small or inconsequential, especially when compared to the magnitude of anticipated moves that normally would induce position traders to enter the market. But sometimes, basis conditions can be sufficiently generous to motivate a trade, simply because the basis offers an attractive edge or cushion to either the short or the long.

The best example of this kind of opportunity comes when no rate trend seems evident or prospects seem equally likely that rates could go up or down over the term to expiration. With this view, the existence of a large basis offers an edge and thus a trading opportunity. Of course, "large" is a relative term, and people may disagree on magnitude; but the key test is whether rates could reasonably be expected to change by as much as the basis within the time period defined by the futures expiration.

As an example, under the same starting conditions as used above (i.e., spot LIBOR at 8.75 percent), assume the view that rates could vary by, say, 50 basis points, up or down. At a price of 91.75 (100 minus 8.25) or higher, selling the futures would be a smart bet; at a price of 90.75 (100 minus 9.25) or cheaper, buying the futures would be the smart bet. In both cases, as long as the rate move were confined to the anticipated range, the trader could expect a best case of making 100 basis points ($2,500) per contract and a worst case of breaking even—a pretty attractive risk/reward prospect.

Further Observations

Finding an attractive basis does not ensure a profitable trade. The movement of spot rates may still overwhelm the basis edge, despite the initial judgment to the contrary. Under such circumstances the trade would result in losses. The basis provides a cushion, but the trade comes with no guarantees. It is a speculative trade—albeit an intelligent one.

This strategy says nothing about fair value. Obviously, it would be nice to have the basis edge reinforced by a "theoretical value edge," but, in fact, the concept of fair value is not relevant to this approach.

Critics of this approach might very well argue that it should be avoided because one is always betting against the consensus forecast indicated by the basis. In truth, one is doing just that, but the forecasting capability of the basis is notoriously poor. The basis is largely a reflection of yield curve conditions— also unreliable indicators of forthcoming rate movements.

The approach presented here is by no means limited to three-month Eurodollar futures. It is a generic concept that can be applied to virtually any futures market. It happens that these contracts frequently post attractive basis conditions, but so do

other contracts. In particular, the newer one-month LIBOR futures warrant close attention. While the trading history has been
quite limited, the opportunities for attractive basis plays have
been rather impressive.

An intelligent trader measures risk versus potential rewards and selectively takes positions where the prospect for
gains outweighs those for losses. The approach suggested here
is offered as one screening device to help in that effort. It is no
panacea, but it may bring some attractive trades to your attention that otherwise might be missed; or, equally valid, it may
steer you away from some losers.

An Historical Perspective

The accompanying chart plots three-month London Interbank
Offered Rates (LIBOR) versus nearby Eurodollar futures rates
(100 minus the closing futures prices). In addition, the difference
between these rates (or the "basis") is also shown on the bottom
portion of the chart. Three independent expiration cycles are
plotted, with the termination of trading in each cycle identified
by the vertical lines in mid-September, mid-December, and mid-
March respectively.

Figure 3–1 highlights three important conclusions: (1) In
general, spot and futures interest rates tend to move together;
(2) the basis appears to be highly variable from expiration cycle
to expiration cycle; and (3) upon the expiration of the futures
contract the basis will be zero.

Mispricing Issues

As an example of the opportunity that arises from mispricings,
consider the abstracted case where the bank's portfolio consists
of a six-month Eurodollar asset (i.e., a placement at another
bank) earning 10 percent, funded by a three-month Eurodollar

Figure 3–1: London Interbank Offered Rates (LIBOR) vs. Eurodollar Futures Rates

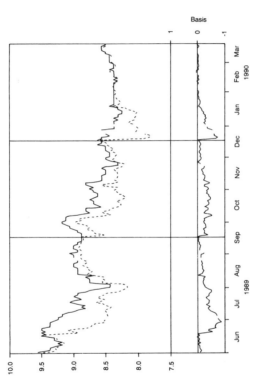

Importantly, this chart gives the very strong impression that interest rates in futures contracts are, and will continue to be, at lower values than the underlying spot market rates. This conclusion, however, is one that should not be expected to exist in general. In fact, the conditions shown reflect the persistence of inverted yield curves over virtually the entire span of time shown. The more usual condition of an upward sloping yield curve will typically cause futures rates to be higher than spot rates.

deposit, secured at 8 percent. By using Eurodollar deposits on both sides of the balance sheet, we can isolate the yield curve effect and keep it apart from the credit concerns of funding with one category or risk while investing in another.

With this starting point, it should be clear that a problem could arise if three-month rates rise by the time of the re-funding. Worth noting, however, is that if the spread or net interest margin is sufficiently positive in the first half of the six-month period, some losses could accrue during the remaining portion, and still the bank might end up with a profit for the whole six-month period.

This break-even rate can be found precisely by using the compounding formula below:

$$\left[1 + R_{L1}\left(\frac{d_1}{360}\right)\right]\left[1 + R_{L2}\left(\frac{d_2}{360}\right)\right] = \left[1 + R_A\left(\frac{d}{360}\right)\right]$$

where

R_{L1} = rate on liabilities during the first portion of the period

d_1 = number of days in the first portion of the period

R_{L2} = rate on liabilities during the second portion of the period

d_2 = number of days in the second portion of the period

R_A = rate on assets over the whole period (i.e., $d_1 + d_2$)

d = $d_1 + d_2$.

To find the break-even rate, consider R_{L2} as the "unknown," plug in all other remaining variables, and solve. In the above example, the break-even rate is 11.8 percent.

Efficient market theorists would argue that in practice, if the futures were under-priced (i.e., a futures rate *above* 11.8 percent), arbitrageurs would borrow for six months, lend for three months, and hedge the second quarter rollover investment; but because of the negative net interest margin in the first quarter (borrowing at 10 percent and lending at 8 percent), the aversion to booking an immediate loss could discourage (understandably) the arbitrage.

Alternatively, if the futures were over-priced (i.e., a futures rate below 11.8 percent) the theory would suggest the opposite arbitrage—that, is borrowing short-term, lending long-term, and hedging the re-financing. In this case, unless the over-pricing were so severe that the futures price was above 90.00, this same negative interest margin issue would inhibit the arbitrage. The only difference would be that the negative interest margin in this latter case would occur during the second quarter rather than the first.

With the yield curve essentially flat, these conditions are likely to preclude much, if any, mispricing of the Eurodollar futures. The above discussion does provide an explanation, however, as to why "mispricing" in these contracts may exist at other times and, importantly, why it may persist for a considerable period. Rather than being a problem, mispricing may be thought of as an opportunity. Specifically, when a futures contract is over-valued (the futures rate is too low) the creation of a synthetic asset or liability incorporating a short futures position will provide a yield advantage over the cash market asset or liability of the same maturity. Conversely, if the futures are undervalued, a synthetic asset or liability constructed with a long futures will provide superior results.

The use of a time line, as shown in the accompanying diagram, facilitates the understanding of how to construct a synthetic asset or liability. It shows a situation where the current date (today) is X days prior to the value date of the next futures contract to expire. An over-priced futures contract suggests that the rate obtained by borrowing Eurodollars for X days and shorting the futures contract as a hedge for a subsequent three-

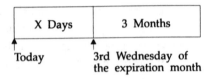

month borrowing will ultimately generate a lower cost of funds than that available in the cash Eurodollar deposit market for the full X days plus three-months period. At the same time, the asset manager can achieve superior results by investing long term and synthetically shortening maturities by selling futures. Conversely, an under-priced futures would suggest that by investing for X days and hedging the subsequent three-month investment period by going long futures, one could beat the X day plus three-month's cash market returns. Or, for the funding manager, funding long with the purchase of a futures (i.e., synthetically shortening the duration of the funding instrument) would enhance performance. Put another way, except for the situation where the futures is priced *precisely* at its break-even value, an opportunity exists for somebody—on one side of the market or the other; but unless you do the evaluation you'll never know if it's for you!

This chapter is based on "Exploiting the Futures Basis," from *Investing,* Fall 1990 and "The (Mis)Pricing of Eurodollar Futures," from *Bonds Asset/Liability Management,* June 1987. Permission granted by *Investing* magazine and Warren, Gorham & Lamont, Inc.

Chapter

4

Introduction to Options Applications with Eurodollar Futures

Although options have long been negotiated in business and financial dealings—probably for centuries—they became formally institutionalized in 1972 with the advent of the Chicago Board Options Exchange. For the first time, options on equity issues were listed as an independent, tradeable financial instrument. Since then, options markets have expanded to include a host of other "underlying instruments," including fixed income securities, currencies, and futures contracts of all sorts. For the most part, options are options, regardless of what the instrument underlying the options happens to be.

In essence, options use falls into one or the other of two categories: Trading and hedging. In the first case, those with no existing price exposure or risk will initiate an options position in the hopes of profiting from correctly anticipating a price adjustment. In the second case, the options are used as an overlay to an existing market sensitivity, such that if an adverse price move develops, the option position will generate an offsetting gain. This chapter first provides a foundation with a discussion of basic options characteristics and nomenclature and then examines each of the alternative uses more closely. It does so in the context of options on Eurodollar futures and interest rate risk management issues. Given this orientation, a brief discussion of the Eurodollar time deposit market and Eurodollar futures will serve as a prelude to the discussion on options.

I. Eurodollar Time Deposits and Eurodollar Futures

The Eurodollar time deposit market is simply a market for dollar denominated bank deposits held outside the continental shores of the United States. Actively quoted markets are made for cash deposits with maturities of overnight, seven-days, one-, two-, three-, six-, nine-months, and one year. Interest accrues on these deposits on the basis of an "actual days" divided by 360 convention. For example, the interest on a $1 million deposit with a maturity of 90 days and of 10 percent would be $1 million × 10 percent × 90/360 = $25,000. London is a major center for trading these deposits and a daily quotation is disseminated from there: the London Interbank Offered Rate or LIBOR. This is the offered side of the Eurodollar deposit market, quoted at 11:00 A.M. London time.

The Eurodollar futures contract sets offered rates on three-month Eurodollar time deposits, commencing on a specific forthcoming date—the third Wednesday of March, June, September, or December, depending on the contract expiration month. Operationally, futures prices are derived by subtracting an interest rate (in percentage points, carried to two decimal places) from 100. Therefore, as interest rates rise, futures prices fall, and vice versa. Every basis point move in the futures price (yield) translates to a cash adjustment of $25. This amount corresponds to the value of a basis point change in yield on a $1 million Eurodollar deposit with a 90-day maturity. In general, movements in the Eurodollar futures market will be closely correlated to yield movements in the underlying Eurodollar time deposit market, though changes will not be precisely equal over any given period of time.

As long as one maintains the futures position—either long (expecting that the market will rise in price, decline in yield) or short (expecting that the market will decline in price, rise in yield)—the participant will be obligated to mark the contract to market and make cash settlements for any changes in value, daily. This obligation can be terminated at any time by simply trading out of the position (i.e., making the opposite transaction). Upon expiration of the contract, any participant still maintaining contracts will have a final mark-to-market adjustment, with the final settlement price based on an average derived from a survey of London bankers who report their perception of the cash market three-month LIBOR at the time of the survey.

II. Foundations of Options

Options come in two types: calls and puts. Calls are the right to buy something at a fixed price. Puts are the right to sell at a fixed price, designated as the "strike" or "exercise" price. Both calls and puts have a limited period for which they are in effect; and the stipulation of this expiration period and the strike price defines each particular instrument. For example, a 89.00-strike June call on a Eurodollar futures contract gives the buyer of this option the right to purchase a June Eurodollar futures contract at a price of 89.00. This right terminates in June, coincidentally with the expiration of the June futures.[1] It should be clear that the right will go unexercised if the June futures can be purchased in the open market for less than 89.00. In this case, this option is called "out-of-the-money." If the market for June futures is trading at a price greater than 89.00, the 89.00-strike call option would be called "in-the-money." And finally, when the futures price equals the strike price, the option is called "at-the-money."

When options are in-the-money, the difference between the strike price and the underlying market price is called "intrinsic value." As long as some time remains before the option expires, the option price, or premium, will likely exceed this intrinsic value, with this excess being referred to as "time value." Importantly, the time value of an option is sensitive not only to the time remaining before expiration, but also to the markets' perception of volatility that is likely to be reflected in the underlying instrument's price during the remaining life of the option. With time remaining, a view that markets will exhibit greater (lesser) volatility will inflate (depress) time value, all other considerations remaining equal.

Often, market participants will speak of the "implied volatility" of an option. This term refers to the measure of volatility that would be used as an input in an option model,[2] such that the theoretical price of an option generated by the model under this assumed volatility equals the options prevailing market price.

When holding options to expiration, a call will make money only if the underlying instrument rises above the strike price plus the price paid for the option; and a put will make money only if the underlying security falls below the strike, less the price paid for the option. In any case, however, the maximum at risk for either the call buyer or put buyer is the price originally paid for the option. At expiration, options on Eurodollar futures are cash settled. That is, both long and short option positions will be offset (or liquidated) at their intrinsic value.

Option buyers pay for their options at the time of purchase. No further cash-flow adjustments are required until either the option is exercised or sold. The option seller, on the other hand, receives the price of the option upon its sale. With exchange traded options, however, the seller must post a margin deposit with the appropriate exchange (via a broker). This margin amount typically will exceed the price of the option. Moreover, if the option appreciates in value, additional margin will likely be required. Conversely if options decline in price, the short option position may be permitted to reduce the value of the posted margin.

In general, call option prices move directly with the price of the underlying instrument and put option prices move inversely with the price of the underlying. The relative price movement of the option as compared to the underlying depends upon the relationship between the underlying price and the exercise price of the option. When an option is deep in-the-money, the option will move almost one-for-one with the underlying price. In this case, we say that the *delta* approaches unity (+1 for calls, –1 for puts).[3] For the case when options are deep out-of-the-money, the relative move of the option with the underlying price (or the *delta*) approaches zero. For at-the-money options, the *delta* is about .5. Importantly, *deltas* also will vary with the time to maturity, as well as with price fluctuations.

Aside from being sensitive to changes in the price of the underlying instrument, *deltas* are also sensitive to time. That is, even if the underlying instrument's price change is stable, *deltas* will change over time. For in-the-money options, the passage of time will increase the absolute value of the delta; and for out-of-the-money options, the passage of time will decrease the absolute value of the *delta, ceteras paribus*.

These sensitivities are shown graphically in the accompanying chart (Figure 4–1). The "zero" on the horizontal scale reflects the at-the-money option. Increasing values to the right reflect movement into-the-money; decreasing values to the left of center reflect movement out-of-the-money. The general "S" shape of the graph becomes increasingly steep as time passes; and this "S" is most extreme at expiration, showing a discrete movement from 0 for any out-of-the-money options to 100 percent for in-the-money options.

The exercise of an option results in the enactment of the right conferred by the option. For example, exercising an option on a futures contract results in the establishment of a futures position. If the buyer of a call option exercises that option, he then will hold a long futures position, initiated at the exercise price. A seller of that call will be assigned a short futures position, also entered at the strike price. Conversely, the buyer of a put position will establish a short futures position at the strike price upon exercise, while a seller of the put will be assigned a long futures position at the exercise price.

III. How Option Traders Trade

Although option trading may be motivated by an expected price move of the underlying instrument, perhaps the majority of professional option traders who buy and sell exchange traded options originate positions because of relative value considerations. In essence, this approach requires the identification of "mispriced" options. Put in a slightly different way, these traders try to identify options with implied volatilities that differ from some expected or forecasted value. An expected rise in implied volatility justifies the purchase of the option (henceforth called the original option position) while an expected decline justifies a sale. In the former case the option would be considered under-priced or cheap; and in the latter case, it would be over-priced or expensive. In both cases, the initiation of an option trade, all by itself, creates an exposure not only to a change in implied volatility but also to a change in the price of the underlying instrument. For trades motivated by the volatility consideration alone, this latter price sensitivity is undesirable. It can be mitigated to a large degree, however, by the imposing of a *delta*-neutral hedge.

The remainder of this section explains (a) how to construct a *delta*-neutral position, (b) how such a position must be monitored and adjusted over time, and (c) what factors could influence the outcome of the trade and foster unexpected results. Treatment of the concept of *gamma* neutrality follows.

For expository purposes, the *delta*-neutral hedging process is initially illustrated with futures contracts used as the hedge vehicle.[4] Assume a trader sells 60 calls on Eurodollar futures with a *delta* of 50% on each call. The *delta* of the portfolio as a whole, then, is simply –60 calls[5] multiplied by .5, or a total of

–30. Put another way, the futures equivalent of this portfolio is 30 short futures. Therefore, the appropriate offset requires buying 30 Eurodollar futures. While correct at the outset, this particular hedge ratio may need to be adjusted if and when the *delta* of the original option changes.

For instance, as the underlying futures price rises (as interest rates fall) the call options will move deeper in-the-money, and thus the *delta* of the portfolio will rise in absolute value, as well. As a consequence, if the original hedge is not altered, the change in the value of the futures position will be insufficient to cover the loss of the original option position. Thus, to hedge appropriately, one would need to adjust the long futures position (a process often referred to as dynamic hedging) by purchasing additional Eurodollar futures as the underlying futures price increases. Unfortunately, if such adjustments were made and the market subsequently reversed itself, the reversal would foster losses on the "extra" hedge position.

In the case of declining futures prices (with rising interest rates), the call options would move deeper out-of-the-money, and therefore the *delta* of the portfolio would decrease in absolute value. As a result, a correct hedge would require a reduction in the size of the long futures position (i.e., the sale of some of the Eurodollar futures initially purchased). Otherwise, losses on the futures position would outpace the profits generated by the short options. As before, a reversal would again foster losses on the adjustment portion of the futures hedge.

Whether the starting position is short calls, as above, or short puts, this conclusion would still apply. That is, in both cases, failure to adjust the hedge when called for would result in losses if a sustained market move were to develop. Moreover, losses would also accrue if adjustments were initiated but market prices ultimately return to (or near) their original levels.

Coupled with these less than sanguine prospects is the fact that the maintenance of a *delta*-neutral hedge is not costless. Costs derive from buying at offered prices and selling at bid prices for all hedge transactions, paying commissions, and outright tracking error because the hedge results fail to match the desired changes in the option prices. On the positive side, the possible saving grace is that in stable markets, these costs will be minimal (hopefully near zero); and as long as the stability persists, the time value of the short options will likely decay, working to the benefit of the short option position taker.

Next, turn to the *delta*-neutral hedge that starts with a long option position, dictated by the presence of an under-priced option. Whether long calls or long puts, failure to adjust the *delta*-neutral hedge when significant price trends arise would prove to be beneficial. As an example, consider an original option position of long calls hedged by short futures. Rising futures prices would foster losses on futures and incrementally larger gains on the calls, because of the rising *delta*. With declining futures prices, gains on the futures would outpace losses on the options, due to the declining *delta*. In other words, with no change in the hedge ratio, as underlying prices trend either up or down, the gradual change in the options *delta* will cause greater gains from one side of the combination position (i.e., the futures or the options) than losses on the other. Perhaps equally attractive, if an adjustment is made to the hedge ratio following a price change (up or down) and a subsequent reversal occurs, this adjustment will involve buying futures low and selling high, or vice versa. Thus, each such reversal will generate incremental trading gains.

These seeming potential benefits, however, may not be overriding. First, the prospect of stable markets again exists; and with the long option starting point, stability means loss of time value. Secondly, even if the adjustments to the hedge do generate trading profits, these gains may not be sufficient to offset the transaction costs associated with the adjustment activity.

It appears that the *delta*-neutralized short options position will benefit from stable markets and suffer with greater volatility; and the reverse is true for the *delta*-neutralized long option position. Transactions costs, however, are adverse to both starting points. Depending on the criteria used for making hedge adjustments, these costs may or may not be directly related to volatility.

From the above discussion, it should be clear that both transaction costs and prospects for tracking error would be reduced if the hedge instruments *delta* automatically adjusted along with the initial options *delta*. This ideal is approached when implementing a *gamma*-neutral hedge.

The *gamma* of an option measures the sensitivity of the *delta* to a change in the price of the underlying instrument. The *gamma* is positive for long option positions (both puts and calls) and negative for short option positions, because higher (lower) futures prices force call *deltas* to become more (less) positive and put *deltas* to become less (more) negative. Moreover, the magnitude of the effect of a given price change on *delta* is greatest for at-the-money options and gets smaller, approaching zero, as the options move deeper and deeper in- or out-of-the-money.

Consider the situation of the option trader interested in minimizing the need for adjustments to his *delta* hedge imposed on a portfolio of option positions. The solution to this problem starts with the calculation of the *deltas* and *gammas* of the portfolio in question. Like the *delta* of the portfolio, the *gamma* of the portfolio is found by adding up the component *gammas*. The portfolios *gamma* would then be neutralized by overlaying a hedge position with an equal and opposite *gamma*.[6] And finally, the last step would be to use futures (for which the *gamma* is zero) to *delta*-neutralize any remaining *delta* on the *gamma*-neutral position.

Realizing the potential for such trades to perform imperfectly, traders would likely initiate them only if the mispricing conditions were sufficiently generous to grant a high probability of success. Put another way, at some sufficiently high price (i.e., implied volatility) it makes sense to sell options on a *delta*- (and *gamma*-) neutral basis; and at another sufficiently low price, it makes sense to be long options, *delta*- (and *gamma*-) neutral. If done properly, some mismatching would likely still arise over time, as *gammas*, like *deltas*, are also somewhat variable. Compared to a futures-only *delta*-neutral hedge, however, a *gamma*-and *delta*-neutral hedge can be expected to offer a second stage of risk protection.

At the same time, because a *gamma*-neutral hedge requires selling options against an original long option position (or buying options against an original short option position), establishing *gamma* neutrality will tend to mitigate both the pros and cons of imposing a futures-only *delta*-neutral hedge. That is, the uncertainty (opportunity as well as risk) associated with the adjustment process will be reduced, as will be the importance of the time value considerations if a *gamma* and *delta*-neutral hedge is put in place, rather than only a *delta*-neutral hedge.

The object of employing a *delta*-neutral hedge is to capture the value of the perceived mispricing of some original option. Such a trade has its risks, however, so some threshold of mispricing must be surpassed to justify undertaking the position. The more conservative the trader, the more extreme these thresholds of mispricing would have to be; and presumably the more infrequently they would occur. Nonetheless, the professional option trader will make these judgments on an ongoing basis and trade when the conditions warrant.

IV. How Risk Managers Hedge

In contrast to the options trader, the hedger has a different time horizon and, as a result, a different approach to using options. The remainder of the chapter demonstrates this approach by examining the case of an institution exposed to short-term interest rate risk. Options on the Eurodollar futures would likely be the instrument of choice for managing this exposure.

Irrespective of the fact that the risk in question may not relate specifically to three-month Eurodollar rates, per se, the number of contracts used for both the futures hedges and static option hedges generally should be determined as follows: Calculate the value of the basis point on the instrument to be hedged and divide by the value of the basis point on the futures contract, or $25. For example, consider the interest rate exposure of a $5 million three-month (90 day) U.S. domestic bank deposit. The value of a basis point would be $125, from $5 million × .0001 × 90/360 = $125. Thus, the correct hedge ratio would be 125/25 = 5 contracts.[7] In contrast, if the deposit had a six-month maturity with the same face value, the value of the basis point would be $250; and the appropriate hedge ratio would be 10 contracts. If concerned about rising rates, the hedger should sell the contracts or go "short"; if worried about falling rates, he should buy or go "long."

Before assessing the possible outcomes, two assumptions are made: First, the hedge is implemented with the correct number of contracts; and second, the hedge is maintained until the rate on the exposure is set, when no further interest rate risk remains. The effective rate realized inclusive of hedge results (Re) would then turn out to be the rate associated with the futures price when the hedge is implemented (Rf1), adjusted by the spread between the spot rate of the exposure (Rs) and the rate implied by the final futures price (Rf2) when the rate setting occurs and the hedge is liquidated. Algebraically,

$$Re = Rf1 + (Rs-Rf2) \qquad (1)$$

The accompanying example shown in Table 4–1 assumes (a) the hedge ratio is calculated using the above described value of a basis point methodology, and (b) the hedge is initiated at a futures price of 92.00, reflecting a rate of 8.00 percent. The exhibit demonstrates outcomes that would result with rising rates (top) and declining rates (bottom). In both cases, three scenarios are shown: Column 1 shows outcomes where deposits are issued at the same rate as the rate associated with the futures price upon liquidation (i.e., Rs–Rf2 = 0); column 2 shows outcomes where deposits are issued at 25 basis points below the liquidation futures rate (Rs–Rf2 = –25); and column 3 shows results when deposits are issued at 25 basis points above the futures rate (Rs–Rf2 = 25). This display demonstrates the validity of equation (1), above, whether interest rates rise or fall or whether the difference in rates at hedge liquidation is due to (a) the spread between spot LIBOR and the spot exposure rate or (b) a non-zero basis of the futures contract.

Besides selling futures, a manager facing the risk of higher interest rates might also consider buying put options or selling call options. Both option strategies would make money if interest rates do, in fact, rise. The two would have different outcomes, however, depending upon the magnitude of the interest rate change. Buying puts allows hedge profits to be generated from rising interest rates; but with rates declining, the loss on the hedge is limited to the price of the options. Put buying may be seen as analogous to purchasing insurance with a deductible clause. A claim can be filed if interest rates rise, and the insurance policy will pay off. Conversely, if interest rates stay the same or fall, the put buyer simply lives with the fact that he paid for insurance but does not file a claim.

Alternatively, suppose the hedger sells calls to protect against rising interest rates. If rates do move higher, the call will lose value. It can then be bought back cheaper, fostering a gain. Thus, with rising rates, the call seller gets to keep some—and perhaps all—of the initial selling price of the options, but no more. If interest rates decline, on the other hand, the option price will rise; and the hedger would be forced to buy back his option position at a higher price and therefore at a loss. Put another way, by choosing this method of coverage, the manager only achieves hedge profits for a limited interest rate increase; but he is completely exposed to an unlimited loss on his hedge if rates unexpectedly decline.

For those who suffer under declining interest rates, all the above solutions are reversed. That is, the choice now becomes buying futures contracts, buying call options, or selling put options. The characteristics are analogous: Futures lock in an effective interest rate[8] and thereby eliminate both risk and opportunity, option buying (calls) offers unbounded hedge profit potential and limited risk, and selling options (puts) offers limited profit potential and unbounded risk.

Whether protecting against rising or falling rates, if the hedge is removed simultaneously with the options' expiration, hedge positions will be offset or liquidated at prices equaling the options' intrinsic value (i.e., the difference between the futures price and the strike price, if beneficial). In contrast, if termination of an options position were to occur prior to the contracts' expiration, the liquidation price would be greater than the intrinsic value, the difference being equal to the options time value. The long option hedger thus benefits by being able to liquidate (sell) his hedge before expiration, while the short option hedger is adversely affected—assuming a given price of the underlying futures.

Returning to the problem posed in Table 4–1, now consider the use of a long put position as a hedge vehicle to protect against the risk of rising deposit rates. Using the same hedge ratio as that calculated for the futures hedge (i.e. 10 contracts), and continuing the assumption that the hedge is maintained until the options expire, put profits will offset higher interest rates—as long as futures prices decline below the strike price of the option.

Figure 4–2 shows results from employing a long 92-put hedge, where the puts are initially purchased at a price of .50. It reflects the assumptions that (a) the options are liquidated with no time value and (b) futures and spot prices (rates) are equal at the time the interest rate is set on the exposure. Figure 4–3 graphs the outcomes associated with the short 92-call hedge, sold at a price of .50, again under those same assumptions. These Figures reveal the fact that long put options offer the same prospective outcomes as do "interest rate caps" or "ceilings," while the calls offer the same results as "interest rate floors."

Relaxation of the two underlying assumptions will alter the effective interest rate realized: For a given spot market interest rate, non-zero basis condition when option positions are liquidated may or may not influence liquidation option prices, depending upon whether or not the intrinsic value of the option is affected. With respect to the time value issue, as noted above, greater time value at hedge termination necessarily benefits long option hedges (i.e., lowers effective interest costs or increases effective returns) and adversely affects short option hedges (i.e., raises interest costs; lowers returns).

At the time a hedge is initiated, it is not clear whether the best results will be generated by using futures contracts, buying options (calls to protect for declining interest rates or puts to protect for rising interest rates), or selling options (the opposite of the long option choices). In fact, depending on how the underlying interest rate changes, any one of the three choices can be the best. The manager's decision should depend on (a) the certainty that the manager attaches to the associated interest rate forecast and (b) the comfort level associated with the potential outcomes of the respective choices. The manager with great confidence in his forecast and an expectation of a sizable adverse interest rate move would be best served by a futures contract. Alternatively, if one expects a large move but has less confidence in the forecast, the long options would likely be preferred. And finally the short option choice would be best when a relatively small adverse rate move is anticipated, but still some cushion of safety is desired.

From the perspective of a hedger, the choices and trade-offs can be stated in the following way: Hedging with futures insulates the hedger from the effects of subsequent interest rate moves—either adverse or beneficial. Buying options is analogous to purchasing insurance for one way protection. And finally, selling options offers a fixed, maximum amount of protection (regardless of the magnitude of an adverse interest rate change) and the prospect of foregoing the positive effects of a beneficial market move. With these basic alternatives understood, the hedge manager can now consider a myriad of alternative strategies that can be developed by combining option positions.

Among the more commonly constructed option combination hedges are collars (also referred to as fences, range-forwards, and cylinders) and vertical spreads. Both are examples of hedges that are designed to offer some degree of protection at a cheaper price than the outright long option hedge.

A collar is nothing more than the purchase of a put (or series of puts) and the sale of a call (or series of calls) to protect against rising interest rates; and the opposite trades to protect against falling rates.[9] In effect, the collar imposes both a floor and a ceiling. Thus, the strike prices of the put (i.e., the ceiling) would always be lower than the strike prices of the call (i.e., the floor). Both of the relevant options would have the same expiration date, and the number of contracts to buy (and sell) would be determined from the value of the basis point method used for sizing the futures hedge.

While a collar appears to foster the security of a worst-case outcome for a cheaper dollar outlay than would be the case for the basic long option hedge, part of the cost of this protection is hidden in the form of an opportunity cost. That is, the short option component of the collar removes the prospect of an unbounded benefit that would otherwise accrue because of a beneficial interest rate move. Thus, the collar leaves the effective interest rate constrained somewhere within best-case/worst-case boundaries.

The vertical spread hedge has the opposite outcome. Within a range of spot interest rates dictated by the strike prices of the component options, the effective rate realized with this hedge is fixed—like the outcome of a futures contract. At both higher and lower interest rates than those specified by the above mentioned range, the hedger is exposed to the effects of further interest rate changes.

Vertical spreads are constructed with the purchase of some original option—puts to protect against rising rates, calls to protect against falling rates—with a coincident sale of a cheaper option of the same type. As before, the options should have the same expiration date; and the number of options bought and sold should be found by the value of a basis point method. Figures 4–4 and 4–5 show the outcome potentials realized by imposing collar and vertical spread hedges, respectively, for a hypothetical hedger concerned about the risk of rising interest rates.[10]

It becomes the manager's responsibility to understand the risks and opportunities associated with the alternative hedge choices available—whether the futures hedge, long options, short options, or some combination of any of the above. No single choice will be right for all situations or all managers. Instead, a business judgment is required, reflecting (a) the inescapable trade-off between price and protection, and (b) the tolerance for uncertainty of outcome, which, to a greater or lesser extent, is inherent in virtually all hedging strategies.

This chapter was written for *Interest Rate Risk Management*, edited by J.C. Francis and A. Wolf, Dow-Jones Irwin, 1993. Reprinted with permission.

Endnotes

1 Not all options expire coincidentally with their underlying futures. Users should consult exchange literature to be clear about expiration schedules and underlying instruments.

2 Volatility is expressed as an annualized standard deviation of rates of change of the underlying price.

3 Some models report *deltas* in percentages, rather than in decimal notation (i.e., 50 percent, rather than 0.5).

4 In fact, one may construct *delta* neutral positions using spot markets, futures, or other options. When constructed with other options, however, one would certainly try to avoid the

sale of options deemed to be under-priced or the purchase of options deemed to be over-priced.

5 A negative sign is required due to the *sale* of these options.

6 This offset can be arranged by any number of option combinations, so the astute hedger would want to be sensitive to relative-value considerations and commission charges that would apply to the various hedge constructs.

7 This approach ignores the issue of present value versus futures value. See Kawaller, "Hedging with Futures Contracts: Going the Extra Mile," *Journal of Cash Management*, June 1986. This article discusses a technique called "tailing," which can be used to remedy this concern.

8 Characterizing futures as "locking in" an effective rate may somewhat overstate these instruments' capabilities in that some minor degree of uncertainty may remain due to basis risk. The issue relates to the prospective uncertainty as to the magnitude of (Rs-Rf2) in equation (1).

9 Generally the proceeds from the options sales are less than or equal to the cost of the long options.

10 These exhibits reflect different option prices than those used in the prior examples.

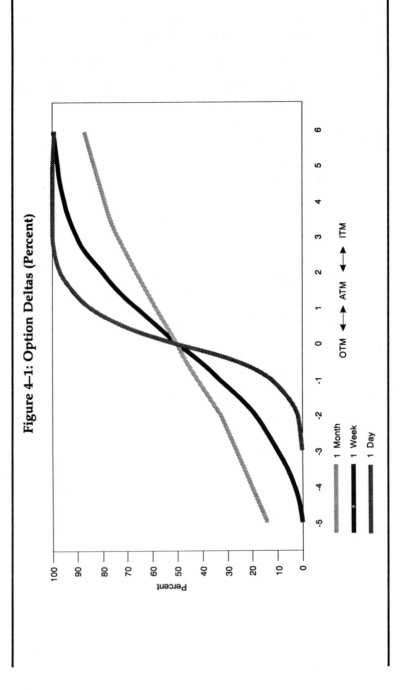

Figure 4-1: Option Deltas (Percent)

Table 4–1: Futures Hedge Examples

Objective: Lock up a funding rate on $15 million 60-day deposits
Hedge Ratio: b.p.v. = $15 million × .0001 × (60/360) = $250
Hedge ratio = $250/$25 = 10 futures (short)
Initial Futures Price: 92.00 (8.00%)

	Outcomes with Rising Rates		
	Rs – Rf2 = 0	Rs – Rf2 = –25	Rs – Rf2 = 25
Liquidation futures price	88.00	88.00	88.00
Rate paid on deposits	12.00%	11.75%	12.25%
Interest paid to depositors	$300,000	$293,750	$306,250
Profit (loss) on hedge	$100,000	$100,000	$100,000
Net interest	$200,000	$193,750	$206,250
Effective interest rate	8.00%	7.75%	8.25%

	Outcomes with Declining Rates		
	Rs – Rf2 = 0	Rs – Rf2 = –25	Rs – Rf2 = 25
Liquidation futures price	95.00	95.00	95.00
Rate paid on deposits	5.00%	4.75%	5.25%
Interest paid to depositors	$125,000	$118,750	$131,250
Profit (loss) on hedge	($75,000)	($75,000)	($75,000)
Net interest	$200,000	$193,750	$206,250
Effective Interest Rate	8.00%	7.75%	8.25%

Figure 4–2: Effective Interest Rates
Long 92.00-Puts

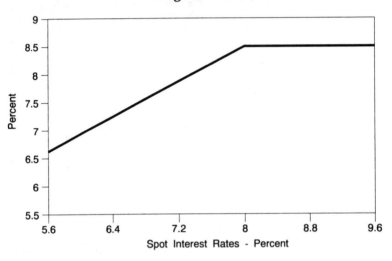

Figure 4–3: Effective Interest Rates
Short 92.00-Calls

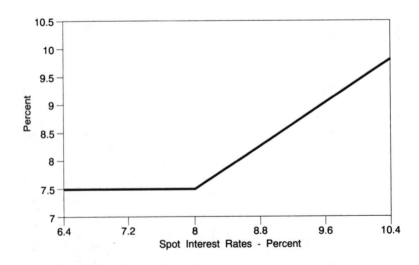

Figure 4–4: Effective Interest Rates
Collar: Long 92.50-Put/Short 93.00-Call

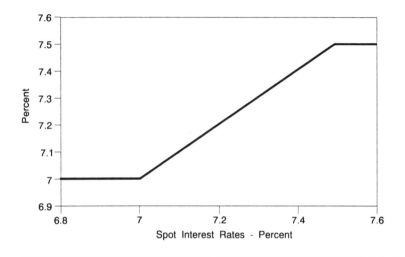

Figure 4–5: Effective Interest Rates
Vertical Spread: Long 92.75-Put/Short 92.25-Put

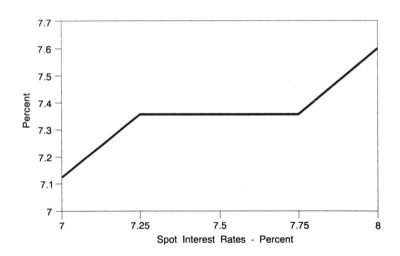

Chapter

5

Stacking vs. Stripping with Eurodollar Futures

W hen repetitive or recurring interest rate exposures call for using Eurodollar futures contracts as hedging instruments, a question arises: Which expiration months should be employed? Two alternative approaches are discussed in this chapter: a stack hedge, wherein the hedger uses only one expiration month, and a strip hedge, wherein contracts are spread over successive months. A methodology is provided to determine which approach is likely to provide the greater benefit.

With the advent of Eurodollar futures contracts, the idea that any company should maintain a passive approach to the potentially devastating consequences of adverse interest rate moves seems anachronistic. In fact, a growing number of financial institutions and corporate treasuries have come to use and appreciate these futures for managing interest rate risk. For bankers, this interest rate exposure could arise from the institution's overall asset/liability gap, positions held by fixed-income trading departments, or capital markets dealing activities. Regardless of the source of the risk, Eurodollar futures have offered an effective mechanism for "fixing" interest rates in advance of rate-setting dates, thereby mitigating—if not eliminating entirely—the potential for detrimental consequences from an adverse interest rate move.

To Stack or Not to Stack

For hedgers with repetitive interest rate exposures (for example, commercial paper issuers, borrowers of variable rate debt, or short-term money managers), the implementation of a futures hedge program raises the question of which contract months to use. Ordinarily, the timing of the exposure dictates the decision. That is, the expiration closest to, and following the rate-setting date for the exposure would probably be the first choice. This selection generally provides the outcome with the smallest degree of basis risk. For repetitive rate-setting problems, this approach would mean the imposition of a "strip" hedge, a hedge constructed using futures with successive expirations. Some situations, however, may call for constructing a "stack" instead, where the hedger uses only one contract expiration month.

As an example, rather than using a strip of 10 September, 10 December, and 10 March contracts, the hedger may prefer to initiate the hedge using 30 September futures under some conditions. Probably the most frequent justification for preferring a stack over a strip hedge relates to liquidity considerations. With more trading concentrated in futures contracts closer to expiration, the more distant months may be characterized by wider bid/ask spreads and smaller quantities bid and offered. As a result, the hedger may sometimes be unable to trade the desired number of contracts in the more distant months without moving the market. For the hedger who sees some potential for terminating a hedge before the projected rate-reset date, this liquidity consideration could be important.

A second consideration for those choosing between stacking and stripping should be price, or more precisely, spread prices. Consider the choice between a four-quarter strip versus a stack on the nearby (March) contract under the following conditions:

Expiration	Price	Spread Price
March	91.00	
		−.10
June	91.10	
		+.15
September	90.95	
		+.05
December	90.90	

*The spread price is calculated as the "near" price minus the "far" price. For example, the March price minus the June price.

Assume the hedger is seeking protection against rising interest rates for exposures of $10 million per quarter for four consecutive quarters, timed roughly and coincidentally with the futures expirations. A strip would require an initial short position of 10 contracts in each of the four consecutive delivery months. Then, at the March rate-setting date, the March contracts would be liquidated (bought back). Upon the reset date in June, the June futures would be liquidated. In turn, the September futures would be liquidated in September. And finally, in December, the December futures would be liquidated.

With a stacking and rolling technique, the hedger typically would start by selling all 40 contracts with the nearby expiration. Then, some time at or before the March expiration, 30 of the 40 contracts would be rolled into the June expiration. That is, one would buy 30 March and sell 30 June futures. The remaining 10 March futures would be liquidated upon the March interest rate setting. Similarly, with the June expiration approaching, 20 futures would be rolled from June to September contracts. The remaining 10 June futures would be liquidated with the June rate-reset, and so on. This process is shown diagrammatically in the top portion of Figure 5–1. For comparison purposes, the stripping process is illustrated in the bottom portion.

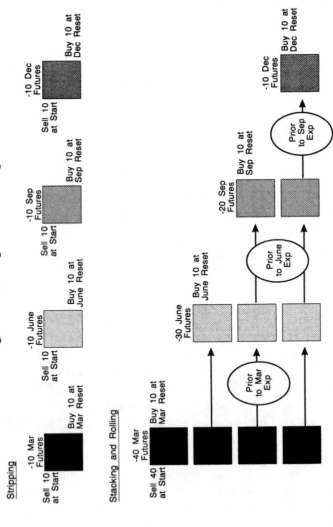

Figure 5–1: Hedge Tactics Diagram

From a dollars-and-cents point of view, determining if it is better to stack or to strip depends on the hedger's expectations: How are the calendar spread prices likely to change over the hedging period? Essentially, this judgment reduces to the question of whether spread prices will become more attractive or less attractive in relation to the initial spread conditions. Stripping locks the hedger into successive interest rates. Stacking and rolling offers the chance to improve performance in relation to the stripping result—or to do worse.

In the case of the conditions described above, the initial spread prices foster a "consolidated spread benchmark" equal to 50 basis points. This value is found by summing the product of the number of contracts rolled, times the initial spread price, for each of the prospective rolls:

30 contracts × –10 basis points	= –300
20 contracts × +15 basis points	= +300
10 contracts × +5 basis points	= + 50
Consolidated spread benchmark	= + 50

The short hedger would choose stripping if he or she believed that the consolidated spread points realized from the prospective roll transactions were likely to be greater than the 50-basis-point benchmark. This outcome would develop if the respective spread prices were to become larger, (that is, more positive or less negative). Otherwise, if the spread prices were expected to become smaller (less positive or more negative), stacking would be preferred.

For the hedger with the opposite risk—the "long hedger"—the criterion would be reversed. Stripping would be preferred if the prospective consolidated spread were expected to decline from the original benchmark.

Unfortunately, one can never be sure in advance what the realized consolidated spread will be. Thus the decision involves a business judgment. Still, there are certain times when stacking would seem to be especially attractive.

For example, the short hedger generally would find stacking in the nearby contract month to be particularly appealing if he or she judged the current consolidated spread benchmark to be especially large (or positive) and unlikely to stay that way. This is likely to be the case during periods of especially upward-sloping yield curves.

In contrast, the long hedger would favor stacking under opposite conditions or when the yield curve is sharply inverted.

Final Considerations

While stripping gives the hedger the greatest certainty of the outcome from imposing a hedge, stacking offers the opportunity for incrementally better hedge results in the form of either larger futures profits or smaller losses. This prospect for enhancement, however, is variable; it changes with market conditions. As a result, the better hedging tactic today may not be the better choice tomorrow. By assessing conditions appropriately, however, the risk manager stands to secure the greatest benefit from the hedging activity.

This chapter is reprinted from *Financial Manager's Statement*, (July/August 1991) with the permission of, and copyrighted 1991 by the Financial Managers Society, Inc., 8 South Michigan Avenue, Chicago, Illinois 60603.

Chapter

6

A Swap Alternative:
Eurodollar Strips

W hether for trading or risk-management purposes, managers may choose between interest rate swaps and strips of Eurodollar futures contracts to meet certain of their objectives. Both allow the conversion of a floating-rate exposure to a fixed rate, or vice versa, thereby increasing or decreasing sensitivity to forthcoming interest rate changes. In the case of the swaps, however, the precise fixed rate in question is readily identifiable. For interest rate strips, on the other hand, the ultimate outcome is more obscure and somewhat uncertain. This chapter is designed to provide a methodology for making direct comparisons between Eurodollar strips and interest rate swaps, to ease the task of identifying the more attractively priced instrument. A brief description of swaps and strips precedes the presentation of the methodology.

Swaps

The standard, or plain vanilla, swap agreement is summarized in Figure 6–1. Here, two counterparties enter into a contract whereby A calculates an interest rate expense obligation based on a floating interest rate benchmark, and B calculates an obligation based on a known fixed rate. Clearly, the amount of the interest expense for which A is responsible will rise in a rising rate environment and fall with declining rates. In contrast, B's obligation is constant, based on the stated, notional amount specified by the swap agreement and the contractually determined fixed interest rate. The swap requires periodic interest payments whereby the net, or difference, between the two interest obligations is passed from the party with the greater obligation to the party with the lesser obligation.

Consider the case where A agrees to pay B based on the London Interbank Offered Rate (LIBOR) on three-month Eurodollar deposits and B agrees to pay A based on a fixed money market rate of 10 percent.[1] Assume a notional amount of $100 million for the swap and quarterly interest payments. With each fixing of LIBOR, A establishes its forthcoming interest obligation. For example, if LIBOR were equal to 10 percent at the first rate setting, no cash adjustment would be made by either party; if LIBOR were 11 percent, counterparty A would pay B $250,000 [($100 million × .11 × ¼) – ($100 million × .10 × ¼)]; and if LIBOR were 9 percent, counterparty B would pay A $250,000 [($100 million × .09 × ¼) – ($100 million × .10 × ¼)]. The same process would continue for the term of the contract, following each quarterly reset of LIBOR.

Assuming both A and B had no exposure to interest rates prior to executing the swap contract, the swap would expose A to the risk of higher short-term rates and the opportunity of

Figure 6–1: Plain Vanilla Swap

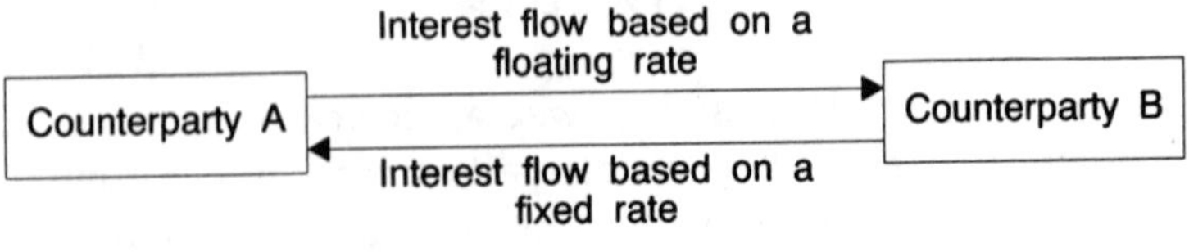

lower rates; B's exposure would be the opposite. Often, however, counterparties will use swaps as an offset for preexisting exposures. In the first case the swap is being used as a trading vehicle, and in the second it is being used as a hedge.

Eurodollar Strips

Strips of Eurodollar futures are simply the coordinated purchase or sale of a series of futures contracts with successive expiration dates. The objective of employing a strip is to lock in a rate of return for a term equal to the length of the strip. For example, a strip consisting of contracts with four successive expirations would lock up a one-year term rate; eight successive contracts would lock up a two-year rate, etc. As is the case with swaps, futures strips may be used either to take on additional interest rate risk in the hopes of making trading profits or as an offset, or hedge, to an existing exposure. A buyer of a Eurodollar futures strip would be equivalent to a fixed-rate receiver on an interest rate swap, and a seller of a Eurodollar futures strip would be equivalent to a fixed-rate payer on an interest rate swap.

In calculating the yield implied in a strip of Eurodollar futures contracts, two questions arise. First, what is the term interest rate that can be expected to result from employing a strip of Eurodollar futures? And, second, how should the hedge be constructed to achieve this rate? In fact, the answer depends on the objectives of the strip creator vis-a-vis the decision on how to treat accruing interest. That is, creation of a synthetic zero coupon, fixed-income security would require one particular hedge construction, while creation of a synthetic coupon-bearing security would require another. To understand all the various alternatives, we start with the case of the zero coupon strip. This methodology is then adopted for the other, perhaps more typical, case.

Consider the problem of creating a one-year zero coupon strip when four successive contract expirations would be used. Assume the prices for these contracts are 92.79, 92.51, 92.27, and 92.05, respectively. Under these conditions, the hedger would have four hedgeable events designed to lock up rates of 7.21 percent (100 - 92.79) in the first quarter, 7.49 percent (100 - 92.51) in the second quarter, 7.73 percent (100 - 92.27) in the third quarter, and 7.95 percent (100 - 92.05) in the fourth quarter. The number of contracts required for the hedge is determined by first determining principal plus interest at the end of each quarter. Assume the number of days in each of the quarters are 91, 91, 91, and 92, respectively. If so, at the end of the first quarter the principal plus interest would be calculated by multiplying the starting principal by the first futures' interest rate (7.21 percent) by 91/360.[2] This end-of-quarter value would become the amount to be hedged to the second quarter, and so on. Table 6–1 assumes an initial value of $100 million.

The number of contracts required is found by taking the value of a basis point for each quarter's opening principal (that is, the prior quarter's ending principal plus interest) divided by $25, or the value of the basis point per futures contract. The actual hedge ratio would have to be rounded to a whole number, of course, as futures cannot be bought or sold in fractional units. The calculations are shown in Table 6–2.

Moving from the specific example to the general methodology, we incorporate the concept of the bond-equivalent yield, which can be derived for a strip of virtually any length (up to the maximum number of quarterly expirations available) from the following formula:

$$\left(1 + RFI\frac{DQ1}{360}\right)\left(1 + RF2\frac{DQ2}{360}\right)\left(1 + RF3\frac{DQ3}{360}\right)$$

$$\cdots\left(1 + RFN\frac{(DQN)}{360}\right) = (1 + ReffP)^{N \times P/4} \tag{1}$$

RF1, RF2, RF3, and *RFN* are the respective annual futures rates (100 minus the appropriate futures prices, expressed as decimals); *DQ1, DQ2, DQ3,* and *DQN* are the days in each of the three-month periods beginning with the third Wednesday of the respective futures' expiration months;[3] *N* is the number of quarters in the strip; *Reff* is the effective annual bond equivalent yield for the strip; and *P* is the number of periods per year for which compounding is assumed.

The left side of Equation 1 shows the effect of borrowing (or lending) for each quarter at the interest rate designated by the appropriate futures contract. The right side incorporates the effective yield that would be required to generate the same principal plus interest by the end of the term. In all cases, effective yields are approximations, since the periods covered by the fu-

Table 6–1: Strip Hedge Objectives

Quarter	Amount Hedged	Quarterly Futures Interest Rate	Days per Quarter	Principal plus Interest (End of Quarter)
1	$100.00 million	7.21%	91	$101.82
2	101.82	7.49	91	103.75
3	103.75	7.73	91	105.78
4	105.78	7.95	92	107.93

Table 6–2: Calculating Hedge Ratios

Quarter	Hedge Ratio Calculations
1	[$100.0 million × (.0001) × $91/360$] /$25 = 101 contracts
2	[$101.82 million × (.0001) × $91/360$] /$25 = 103 contracts
3	[$103.75 million × (.0001) × $91/360$] /$25 = 105 contracts
4	[$105.78 million × (.0001) × $92/360$] /$25 = 108 contracts

tures contracts may either overlap or have gaps.[4] Despite the fact that futures expire quarterly, one may calculate an effective term rate assuming any compounding frequency. Most likely, the choice of P would reflect the compounding assumptions implicit in the fixed-rate quotation of an instrument to which the strip yield may be compared.

Returning to the conditions in the above example where a one-year strip was arranged with contracts priced at 92.79, 92.51, 92.27, and 92.05, respectively, the target one-year return is 7.93 percent.[5] To demonstrate the robustness of this hedge, two extreme cases are shown. End-of-quarter balances are found by investing the initial $100 million at the spot LIBOR, but adjusting the ending principal plus interest by the gains or losses on that quarter's hedge. Such practice is consistent with the accounting tradition of allocating hedge results to the quarter for which the hedge is designed. On a cash flow basis, however, hedge gains and losses for all contracts are generated daily with the variation margin adjustments. Returns calculated from actual cash flows, therefore, would differ from the calculations shown.

In the first case (Table 6–3) it is assumed that LIBOR immediately skyrockets to 15 percent and remains there, following the initiation of the hedge. Thus all futures are liquidated at 85.00. In the second case (Table 6–4) it is assumed that LIBOR drops to 2 percent and remains there; thus all futures are liquidated at 98.00. Both cases result in identical ending balances, demonstrating the robustness of the hedge.

Real World Considerations

Despite the apparent precision shown, it should be recognized that the analysis assumes perfect convergence between LIBOR and the Eurodollar futures rate each time a futures contract expires or is liquidated. In fact, a non-zero basis at the time of

Table 6–3: Case 1: Interest Rates Rise to 15 Percent

Quarter	Futures Results
1	101 contracts × (85.00 − 92.79) × $2,500 = −$1.97 million
2	103 contracts × (85.00 − 92.51) × $2,500 = −$1.93 million
3	105 contracts × (85.00 − 92.27) × $2,500 = −$1.91 million
4	108 contracts × (85.00 − 92.05) × $2,500 = −$1.90 million

Quarter	End of Quarter Balances
1	$100.0 million (1 + .15 × 91/360) − $1.97 million = $101.82 million
2	$101.82 million (1 + .15 × 91/360) − $1.93 million = $103.75 million
3	$103.75 million (1 + .15 × 91/360) − $1.91 million = $105.78 million
4	$105.78 million (1 + .15 × 92/360) − $1.90 million = $107.93 million

*As prices are reflective of percentage points, rather than basis points, the multiplier becomes $25 × 100, or $2,500. Positive values indicate gains; negative values indicate losses.

Table 6–4: Case 2: Interest Rates Decline to 2 Percent

Quarter	Futures Results
1	101 contracts × (98.00 − 92.79) × $2,500 = $1.32 million
2	103 contracts × (98.00 − 92.51) × $2,500 = $1.41 million
3	105 contracts × (98.00 − 92.27) × $2,500 = $1.50 million
4	108 contracts × (98.00 − 92.05) × $2,500 = $1.61 million

Quarter	End of Quarter Balances
1	$100.0 million (1 + .02 × 91/360) + $1.32 million = $101.82 million
2	$101.82 million (1 + .02 × 91/360) + $1.41 million = $103.75 million
3	$103.75 million (1 + .02 × 91/360) + $1.50 million = $105.78 million
4	$105.78 million (1 + .02 × 92/360) + $1.61 million = $107.93 million

hedge liquidations could alter the results.[6] The size of this effect, of course, depends on the magnitudes and directions of the basis upon liquidation. For the long strip (that is, where the futures contracts are originally purchased), a desirable liquidation basis is one where LIBOR is higher than the rate implied by the futures contract. An undesirable basis upon liquidation is one where LIBOR is below the futures rate. For the short strip, the opposite characterizations apply. A worthwhile exercise assumes a worst-case basis, based on possible adverse market conditions that might apply when the futures contracts are liquidated.[7]

Returning to Case 1 as an example, and assuming a long strip was created with LIBOR at 15 percent, assume the worst case of futures liquidation at 84.75, or a rate of 15.25 percent for each futures contract. The worst-case projected results differ from the previous results because of the somewhat greater futures losses in each quarter—the differences equaling the number of contracts for that quarter's hedge times 25 basis points times $25 per basis point, as shown in Table 6-5.

Table 6–5: Worst-Case Scenario

Quarter	Futures Results
1	101 contracts × (84.75 − 92.79) × $2,500 = −$2.03 million
2	103 contracts × (84.75 − 92.51) × $2,500 = −$2.00 million
3	105 contracts × (84.75 − 92.27) × $2,500 = −$1.97 million
4	108 contracts × (84.75 − 92.05) × $2,500 = −$1.97 million

Quarter	End of Quarter Balances
1	$100.0 million $(1 + .15 \times {}^{91}\!/_{360})$ − $2.03 million = $101.76 million
2	$101.76 million $(1 + .15 \times {}^{92}\!/_{360})$ − $2.00 million = $103.62 million
3	$103.62 million $(1 + .15 \times {}^{91}\!/_{360})$ − $1.97 million = $105.58 million
4	$105.58 million $(1 + .15 \times {}^{92}\!/_{360})$ − $1.97 million = $107.65 million

Because of the greater futures losses, a return of 7.65 percent results, rather than a bond-equivalent yield of 7.93 percent as initially targeted. Given the subjective nature of the estimate of the worst case circumstance, however, a more judgmental approach may be incorporated at this stage. The above calculation demonstrates that the adverse basis of 25 basis points at each hedge liquidation lowers the perfect convergence target by 28 basis points (7.93 percent - 7.65 percent)—just about one for one. Importantly, the magnitude of this anticipated liquidation basis is judgmentally determined, and in many cases this actual outcome is likely to be substantially smaller than that just shown. For example, this effect could be virtually negligible in the case where hedges are scheduled for liquidation at or near futures' expiration dates. It should also be realized that the basis conditions upon the hedge liquidation may be favorable, in which case the hedge performance would be better than that indicated by the perfect convergence calculation.

Extensions and Refinements

When considering the strip as an alternative to another fixed-income security, one should try to arrange the strip so it mirrors the cash flow properties of the competing instrument as closely as possible. As an example, if the alternative to the strip is a two-year swap where the fixed payments are scheduled semiannually, the strip should be formulated to replicate semiannual cash disbursements.

To clarify the process, think about the two-year, fixed-income obligation as if it were a series of four, six-month zero coupon strips, where the bond-equivalent yield of each six-month strip would be calculated and implemented as explained in the previous section. The effective rate for the whole two-year period would reflect compounding of all substrip segments. The appropriate general formula follows:

$$(1 + BEY1/P)^t (1 + BEY2/P)^t \cdots (1 + BEYk/P)^t = (1 + R/P)^{Kt} \quad (2)$$

where   BEYi = the bond-equivalent yield of the ith substrip.

   P = the assumed number of compounding periods per year,

   t = length of each substrip in compounding periods,

   K = the number of substrips,

   R = the annualized yield to maturity

For illustrative purposes, consider the prices in Table 6–6 relevant to the above synthetic two-year, semiannual-coupon, fixed-income construction.

Days per quarter are counted rigorously, from the third Wednesday of the expiration month to that calendar day three months later, and the two-quarter strip yields are calculated using the methodology of Equation 1.[8] Next, using the bond-equivalent yield from Table 6–6 and incorporating equation (2), one can find the annualized yield to maturity R. In this case R = 9.18 percent.

The final step needed to realize this outcome is to set up the hedge properly. As this synthetic construction is designed to mimic a security with semiannual coupons, the amount to be hedged in the first, third, fifth, and seventh quarter will be the notional amount of the deal. Assuming a $100-million deal, given the respective days in each of these quarters, the hedge ratios are 100, 100, 102, and 100 contracts, respectively (see Table 6–7). For the remaining quarters (two, four, six, and eight) the calculation takes the original notional amount plus the interest income from the prior quarter, based on that quarter's futures rate. That is, the hedge ratio for the second quarter depends on the futures rate locked up in the first quarter, the hedge ratio for the fourth quarter depends on the third quarter's futures rate, and so on. These calculations are shown in Table 6-7.

As was the case with the zero coupon strip construction, the actual outcomes may differ somewhat from the calculated target due to rounding errors and the prospect of imperfect convergence. Thus we should give appropriate allowance for some

Table 6–6:
Futures Prices and Board Equivalent Yields (BEYs)

Contract Expirations	Futures Price	Days per Quarter	BEY Two-Quarter Strips
1	91.22	90	
2	91.34	92	8.91
3	91.21	90	
4	91.04	92	9.08
5	90.87	92	
6	90.90	91	9.37
7	90.82	90	
8	90.75	91	9.37

Table 6–7: Hedge Construction: $100 Million Semiannual Coupons and Two-Year Maturity

Quarter	Hedge Ratio	
1	$100 million × .0001 × $90/360/25$ =	100
2	$100 million × (1 + .0878 × $90/360$) × .0001 × $92/360/25$ =	104
3	$100 million × .0001 × $90/360/25$ =	100
4	$100 million × (1 + .0879 × $90/360$) × .0001 × $92/360/25$ =	104
5	$100 million × .0001 × $92/360/25$ =	102
6	$100 million × (1 + .0913 × $92/360$) × .0001 × $91/360/25$ =	103
7	$100 million × .0001 × $90/360/25$ =	100
8	$100 million × (1 + .0918 × $90/360$) × .0001 × $91/360/25$ =	103

deviation from these calculations when determining whether or not to choose a strip as the preferred transaction vehicle. With these considerations in mind, failure to choose the alternative with the more (most) attractive yield necessarily leaves money on the table and thus reflects a suboptimal market decision.

Strips versus Swaps

It should be clear from the above discussion that the Eurodollar strip may substitute for interest rate swaps in certain cases. It may not be suitable to make the substitution in all cases, however. Specifically, the primary constraint is the length of the futures expiration cycle. Currently, the Eurodollar expirations extend for four years, suggesting that Eurodollar strips may best be used in conjunction with or in place of relatively short-term interest rate swaps (i.e., swaps with less than a four-year term). For longer terms, one might be tempted to take temporary futures positions in available expirations and then roll these trades into the appropriate month, once they become available for trading. This strategy, however, may be somewhat risky, as the relative prices in place at the time of the roll will vary with changing yield curve positions. Importantly, this risk may also turn out to be an opportunity, as the outcome may yield more, rather than less, desirable results.

Aside from the pure price considerations, some other institutional aspects of futures versus swaps should be appreciated by potential users:

1. Because they are principal-to-principal transactions, swaps can be tailored to meet the individual needs of the counterparties, reflecting very specific timing and exposure characteristics. In contrast, Eurodollar futures are standardized with respect to both timing and dollar values.

2. The arrangement of a swap involves a single transaction at its inception. Futures require periodic subsequent transactions as well. That is, at each rate-fixing date, those contracts designed to hedge that specific exposure need to be liquidated or offset. Thus, futures require more ongoing maintenance and managerial effort than do swaps.

3. A secondary managerial difference deals with cash-flow characteristics of the two alternatives. The daily marking to market, required by futures but not by swaps, may result in cash inflows or outflows with associated profit and tax implications. The former case enhances the economics of the deal, while the latter case detracts. In addition, the harder to measure managerial costs of handling this cash-flow obligation are associated with futures but absent for swaps.

4. Bid-ask spreads will vary in the swap market, depending on the identity of the counterparty. Greater acceptance in the marketplace will mean more liquidity and thus tighter spreads. In contrast, standardization of Eurodollar futures allows for significantly tighter bid-ask spreads.

5. Each swap deal requires a separate settlement and documentation for each counterparty. Thus the first deal with any new counterparty requires substantial preliminary work and legal attention. For futures, once the broker/customer agreement is signed, the whole market becomes accessible, virtually instantaneously.

6. With futures, buying and selling (or initiating and liquidating) positions is equally easy, with no market penalty or widening of bid-ask spreads associated with an offsetting transaction. This may not be the case with swaps. Reversing a swap will typically require some

accommodation by the counterparty, for which there is likely to be a market impact.

7. With a swap on the books, the risk of default is ever present, and the cost of nonperformance may be considerable. In contrast, with exchange-traded futures, the credit exposure rests with the clearing house, and daily marking to market and cash settlement practices serve virtually to eliminate the kind of counterparty risk associated with swaps.

Conclusion

Though swaps and Eurodollar strips each have their own special features or characteristics, they are perhaps more similar than they are different. Each can be used to convert a fixed-rate exposure to floating, or vice versa; each can be used for trading or hedging purposes; and each can serve as an offset, or hedge, for the other. The most intelligent use of the markets, therefore, allows for using the two markets, choosing the more attractive whenever the need exists.

Constructing Eurodollar strips requires a certain amount of care and tailoring in order to make proper comparisons with alternative instruments. Inappropriate yield calculations and improper hedge implementation obviously could cause either the incorrect choice or unexpected results. Whenever employing a strip, one should try to match the cash flow provisions of the competing alternative instrument as closely as possible. The payoff for making this calculation correctly and implementing it properly is achieving incrementally superior returns. Certainly, choosing the more attractively priced alternative will necessarily enhance performance.

This chapter is reprinted from *Interest Rate Swaps*, Carl R. Beidlemen (ed.), 1990. Used with permission. This chapter is largely based on a prior published work: "Interest Rate Swaps versus Eurodollar Strips," *Financial Analysts Journal*, September-October 1989.

Endnotes

1 Often the terms of the swap will relate the fixed rate to some benchmark (e.g., 300 basis points above the rate for five-year U.S. Treasury securities). This practice allows a general swap agreement to be worked out where the pricing details will reflect market conditions at the time the deal is signed.

2 The denominator 360 reflects the convention that LIBOR is quoted as a money market rate, counting the actual number of days during the period in the numerator.

3 One should measure the number of days in the quarter by counting from the calendar day of the third Wednesday of the expiration month to that same calendar day, three months later (e.g., March 17 to June 17, which measures 92 days).

4 That is, the value date of Eurodollar futures contracts is always the third Wednesday of the contract month, and the underlying instrument is the three-month deposit that would mature three months later, on the same calendar day. That maturity day, however, may not coincide with the value date of the subsequent futures. For example, the value date of the March futures might be March 18, while the value date of the June futures might *not* be the 18th. If the third Wednesday of June were earlier, the cycle would result in some overlap of the hypothetical deposits. On the other hand, if the value date were later, the cycle would result in some gaps.

5 This result follows from an ending principal plus interest of $107.93 million, one year after an initial principal of $100 million. It assumes P = 1.

6   The basis is the difference between the spot market price (or rate) and the futures market price (or rate).

7   The existence of gaps or overlaps due to the futures expiration cycle can be considered as a special case contributing to this risk.

8   P of Equation 1 is assumed to reflect semiannual compounding for these calculations.

Chapter

7

Playing the Yield Curve with LIBOR and Eurodollar Futures

U sing LIBOR and Eurodollar futures,[1] a host of alternative trades can be constructed, each focusing on two distinct points on the yield curve. Some of these trades are rather easy to conceptualize and to construct; others are somewhat more esoteric and cumbersome. Still, depending on the prevailing market conditions, the prospective rewards may justify the effort.

Perhaps the most straightforward strategy involves trading LIBOR futures against Eurodollar futures on a one-to-one basis—the LED spread. This trade relates strictly to the one-month and three-month points on the yield curve. If expecting one-month rates to fall relative to three-month rates, buy the LIBOR and sell the Eurodollar futures. With opposite expectations, do the reverse.

A second trade idea involves trading either the nearby LIBOR or the nearby Eurodollar futures against strips of various lengths composed of successive one-month contracts or successive three-month contracts.[2] Thus, the capability exists to trade one- or three-month rates against discrete points in the yield curve, extending out to four years (16 quarters).

Here's how: Suppose your analysis leads you to believe that the yield curve, currently upward sloping, is likely to flatten; and, in particular, the points at the three-month and two-year maturities offer the greatest profit potential. You would want to sell the nearby Eurodollar (henceforth called contract #1, with successive contracts to be referred to as contracts #2, #3, #4, etc.) and buy the two-year strip, composed of contracts #1 through #8.[3] The proper proportion requires a minimum trade of selling eight of the contract #1 and buying one each of contracts #1 through #8. The net effect of this trade would then be selling seven of contract #1 and buying single contracts #2 through #8 (i.e., the first contract of the strip offsets one of the nearby futures contracts), as shown below:

Contract	3-month	2-year	Consolidation
#1	8 short	1 long	7 short
#2	0	1 long	1 long
#3	0	1 long	1 long
#4	0	1 long	1 long
#5	0	1 long	1 long
#6	0	1 long	1 long
#7	0	1 long	1 long
#8	0	1 long	1 long
Total	8 short	8 long	7 short and 7 long

In the above trade, one would expect to make (or lose) approximately $200 for each basis point adjustment of the spread between three-month and two-year rates (i.e., 8 × $25 = $200).

This concept can be further generalized. Suppose, for example, you expect the flattening of the yield curve to be most dramatic over the range between one year and two-and-a-half years, again assuming an initial, upward sloping yield curve. In this case, you would want to sell a one-year strip (i.e., the first four contracts) and buy a strip of contracts #1 through #10. In order to balance the number of contracts bought and sold, the minimum trade would require selling five each of contracts in the one-year strip and buying two each of the contracts in the two-and-a-half year strip. The consolidation of this trade follows:

Contract	1-year Strip	2½-year Strip	Consolidation
#1	5 short	2 long	3 short
#2	5 short	2 long	3 short
#3	5 short	2 long	3 short
#4	5 short	2 long	3 short
#5	0	2 long	2 long
#6	0	2 long	2 long
#7	0	2 long	2 long
#8	0	2 long	2 long
#9	0	2 long	2 long
#10	0	2 long	2 long
Total	20 short	20 long	12 short and 12 long

Here, each basis point adjustment in the spread would foster a $500 effect (i.e., 20 × $25 = $500).

A final strategy that allows operating at even more distant points on the yield curve uses LIBOR or Eurodollar contracts (either individual contracts or strips) traded against Chicago Board of Trade (CBT) government note or bond contracts. The sizing of such trades involves equating the value of a basis point move on both sides.

For CBT contracts, this basis point value is variable, found by (a) determining that instruments basis point value for a $100,000 face amount of the cheapest to deliver instrument (by calculating the price effect of a one basis point change in the yield to call), and (b) multiplying this basis point value by the bond or notes CBT factor. The proper trade proportion is found by the following equation:

$$\frac{BPV_{CBT}}{\$25} = \frac{\#CME}{\#CBT}$$

Where   BPV$_{CBT}$ = the basis point value of the CBT futures
            #CME = the number of CME futures
            #CBT = the number of CBT futures

To illustrate this strategy, suppose you wanted to trade a one-year Eurodollar strip against the CBT five-year note contract. Assume the cheapest to deliver note has a CBT factor of 0.9910 and a basis point value of $42.20. Under these assumptions, the CBT note futures would be expected to generate slightly less than $42 per basis point change in interest rates ($42.20 × .9910 = $41.82). Because a four-quarter Eurodollar strip can be expected to generate about $100 for the same rate move, an appropriate construction would balance five note contracts against two, one-year Eurodollar strips (eight Eurodollar futures, total).[4] Some rounding error should be tolerated, however. With such a combination, if the spread between the two relevant interest rates diminishes, as expected, the trade should generate profits, based on the difference between these two respective interest rates, regardless of whether rates move generally higher or lower. Put another way, any rate move that leaves the relevant rate spread at or about its original magnitude should have no significant profit or loss, except for that amount attributable to rounding error.

Part of the attractiveness of understanding the technology presented in this article is that these trades generally tend to be somewhat less risky than outright interest rate futures positioning. That is, yield curve shifts typically develop more gradually and exhibit fewer "shocks" than are found with singular points on the yield curve. As a result, many experienced traders make the judgment that it is easier to discern yield curve trends than it is to forecast movements in individual rates. The kind of trades discussed above simply allow profits to be made by those traders who *are* able to anticipate these yield curve shifts correctly. Using these procedures, those traders are in a position to profit from their capabilities.

©1992, Chicago Mercantile Exchange

Endnotes

1   The accepted convention recognizes "LIBOR" futures as the CME contract that pertains to a $3 million one-month Eurodollar time deposit, and the "Eurodollar" futures refers to the contract with a $1 million face value, three-month Eurodollar deposit. The convention is somewhat unfortunate as both contracts are used to "lock-in" the offered rates of the respective terms.

2   In calculating the effective strip rate, the money market rates of the strips component contracts should be compounded, rigorously accounting for the precise number of days between the respective futures value dates. This methodology is demonstrated in Chapter 6.

3   The "nearby" Eurodollar refers to the contract with the nearest expiration. If the nearby contract is scheduled to expire prior to the expected market adjustment, however, one should adjust the strategy by using contract #2 versus a strip composed of contracts #2 through #9.

4   Due to the property of convexity, the interest rate sensitivity of bond/note futures is not stable, such that the appropriate proportions for this trade may vary as interest rates change.

Chapter

8

Tactical Considerations in Managing Short-Term Interest Rate Hedges

(with Timothy W. Koch)

The choice of futures contract in establishing a hedge is generally dictated by the specific cash interest rate for which hedging is desired. The preferred contract is the one that exhibits the highest correlation with interest rate movements of the underlying exposure. When several contracts demonstrate acceptable degrees of correlation, however, traders have an incentive to identify the most attractively priced instrument and may further benefit by shifting their positions among instruments throughout the hedge. The purpose of this chapter is to demonstrate that hedges based on a simple trading rule would have enhanced overall performance with short-term T-bill and Eurodollar futures from 1985 through 1989. The implication is that hedge substitution may be an attractive tactical managerial device compared to the traditional "place-and-hold" hedge practice.

The trading rule offered involves comparing three-month T-bill and Eurodollar futures prices to the prices of their underlying instruments. A relative value preference is established whenever the difference between the futures spread and cash spread exceeds certain thresholds. This is similar to the rule employed by Eaker and Grant (1990) in managing foreign exchange hedges. We conducted several simulations following the format of MacDonald, Peterson, and Koch (1988), to analyze potential incremental profits available to participants who manage a hedge based on the trading rule. The results indicate that participants who use even this simple trading rule can, on average, improve hedge performance.

I. Selecting the Hedge Instrument

Consider the hedger who wants to protect the risk of a short-term interest rate exposure. Both three-month T-bill and Eurodollar futures contracts satisfy the correlation requirements imposed by accounting regulators because the two underlying cash rates are highly correlated. In such a case, it seems reasonable to assess the relative values of the contracts before implementing a hedge. If a short hedge were needed, the hedger would prefer to sell the one deemed relatively more expensive. Conversely, a hedger with a need to be long in futures would prefer the cheaper of the two contracts.

In this context, the designation of relatively expensive or cheap refers to the expectation of an impending price adjustment and not a simple comparison of prices, per se. Specifically, if a trader expected Eurodollar futures prices either to rise faster or decline more slowly than T-bill futures prices, Eurodollar futures would be relatively cheaper and T-bill futures relatively more expensive. If Eurodollar futures were expected to fall faster or rise more slowly, they would be relatively more expensive than T-bill futures.

The difficulty is, of course, finding an objective criterion that correctly identifies the contract that is over- or underpriced. Our approach compares the difference between the T-bill futures price and corresponding Eurodollar futures price, the TED spread, with the coincident difference between the two prices on the underlying three-month T-bill and three-month Eurodollar cash securities. The motivation is straightforward. Both T-bill and Eurodollar futures prices converge to prices that reflect their underlying cash rates at expiration of the futures contracts. The TED spread should similarly converge to its cash spread.[1] Thus, when differences arise between the TED spread and its cash counterpart, a seeming advantage accrues to one hedge instrument versus the other.

Consider the case in which the cash spread, LIBOR minus the discount rate on three-month T-bills, equals 100 basis points, while the TED spread equals 125 basis points. In a steady-state environment in which cash rates remain constant, or as long as the two cash quotations move by equal amounts in the same direction, the Eurodollar futures price will necessarily rise in relation to the T-bill futures price over time as the cash spread and TED spread converge.[2] As a result, a positive disparity between the TED spread and cash spread suggests an attractive time for hedgers to prefer buying Eurodollar futures for any long hedge or selling T-bill futures for a short hedge. A negative disparity justifies the opposite preferences. Formally, the trading rule is:

1. When TED > CSD, buy Eurodollar futures (or sell T-bill futures),

2. when TED < CSD, buy T-bill futures (or sell Eurodollar futures),

where   TED = three-month Eurodollar futures rate minus the three-month T-bill futures rate (T-bill futures price minus the Eurodollar futures price), and

CSD = three-month Eurodollar cash rate minus the three-month T-bill cash rate.

While the difference between the TED spread and cash spread signifies a probable change in relative rates, beneficial hedge results are clearly not guaranteed. First, the existing discrepancy could worsen before it improves. Second, the cash spread could change to match the TED spread in such a way that the expected futures rate adjustment does not arise. To protect against these pitfalls, a safety margin should be built into the rule for adopting an alternative hedge instrument. In the following section, we introduce a simulation procedure that incorporates such a safety margin through the use of filters that specify a minimum disparity before taking a futures position.

II. Simulation Results for Alternative Hedge Instrument Opportunities

We use a simulation procedure to examine whether the choice of hedge instrument systematically generates incremental hedge profits or diminished hedge losses when compared to the results otherwise available to traders who follow a simple, single instrument hedging strategy. Identical results follow whether the problem is framed in terms of opportunities to substitute long Eurodollar futures for long T-bill futures or opportunities to substitute short T-bill futures for short Eurodollar futures. Our presentation arbitrarily assumes that the use of T-bill futures is the "control" strategy and Eurodollar futures serve as a potential substitute. We perform our evaluation for both a long hedger and a short hedger. Identical results would appear if the Eurodollar hedge were treated as the control and T-bill futures were substituted. Put another way, the results appropriate for the substitution of long Eurodollar futures for long T-bills is identical to the results appropriate for substituting short T-bills for short Eurodollars.

Using the previous notation, the first strategy examined consists of making long Eurodollar/short T-bill substitutions if TED > CSD. To provide a safety margin, the substitution is initiated only when the difference (TED – CSD) exceeds some threshold; it is reversed when the difference erodes to a base level. In the following analysis, three threshold filters are used: 25, 20, and 15 basis points, respectively. The base level for offsetting the hedge is fixed at 10 basis points. Specifically, a long hedge substitution is initiated when TED-CSD ≥ 25 basis points and is reversed as soon as TED-CSD ≤ 10 basis points. The trader is assumed to implement another hedge substitution when the initial filter is again met. The simulation procedure is then replicated by lowering the threshold to 20 basis points and finally 15 basis points, with the same 10 basis point base level.

In each sequence where a substitution is indicated, the incremental hedge profit is measured as the difference between the hedge profit from Eurodollar futures and the hedge profit from T-bill futures.

Letting EF_t = three-month Eurodollar futures price at time t when a hedger initiates the substitution,

EF_{t+n} = three-month Eurodollar futures price at time t+n when a hedger terminates the substitution,

TF_t = three-month T-bill futures price at time t when a hedger initiates the substitution, and

TF_{t+n} = three-month T-bill futures price at time t+n when a hedger terminates the substitution;

Thus, the incremental hedge profit (PRL) for the long Eurodollar futures substitutions or the short T-bill substitution equals:

$$PRL = (EF_{t+n} - EF_t) - (TF_{t+n} - TF_t)$$

The second strategy consists of substituting short Eurodollar futures or long T-bill futures if TED < CSD. To provide a similar safety margin this hedge is initiated according to three filters specifying initial thresholds with TED-CSD less than or equal to -25, -20, and -15 basis points, respectively, and a base level of TED-CSD greater than or equal to -.10 when the substitution is reversed. Using the previous notation for Eurodollar and T-bill futures prices, but designating i as the point in time when a substitution is initiated and i+n when a hedger returns to the original futures hedge, the incremental hedge profit from this sequence of trades (PRS) can be expressed as:

$$PRS = (EF_i - EF_{i+n}) - (TF_i - TF_{i+n})$$

The simulation was conducted for the 20 nearby Eurodollar and T-bill futures contracts over the period from January 1985 through December 1989, during which interest rates both rose and fell. The data include daily closing rates on three-month Eurodollar and T-bill futures, and three-month Eurodollar and T-bill cash quotes.[3]

Consider first the Table 8–1 results, in which hedgers substitute long Eurodollar futures or short T-bill futures because the TED spread exceeds the cash spread. The first column indicates the three different filters used, starting with the most restrictive 25-basis-point differential threshold. The next five columns record the number of trades, with the fraction of profitable substitutions in parentheses, and data on the minimum profit, maximum profit, mean profit, and total profit, respectively. The final two columns present the probability that the mean profit is less than or equal to zero based on a one-tailed t-test, and the Wilcoxon Z-value for a Wilcoxon matched pairs signed rank test.[4] The null hypothesis for the Wilcoxon test is again that the incremental hedge profit (PRL) is less than or equal to zero.

The results presented in Table 8–1 vary across filters. With the most restrictive 25-basis-point differential in the TED spread versus cash spread, the mean incremental hedge profit is just under seven basis points per substitution, ranging from a 22-

basis-point loss to a 50-basis-point gain. The hypothesis that the incremental profit is less than or equal to zero is rejected with both a t-test and Wilcoxon signed-rank test at the 5 percent level. Of the 44 substitutions, 23, or 54.5 percent, were profitable. In general, the magnitudes of the beneficial effects tend to be larger than the magnitudes of the detrimental ones.

Not surprisingly, incremental hedge profits decline with less restrictive filters. With a 20-basis-point threshold, the number of hedge substitutions increases to 63, with 54 percent profitable. The mean incremental profit is again significantly greater than zero, but it declines to approximately 5 basis points. Under the lowest 15-basis-point threshold, the mean incremental profit is not statistically different from zero at the 5 percent level. The dollar amount of profits under the various filters, assuming a substitution at each trigger and ignoring transactions costs, range from $6,000 with the least restrictive filter to $7,875 with the middle filter.[5]

The results in Table 8-2 summarize the outcomes when hedgers initially substitute short Eurodollar futures or long T-bill futures. Notice that the number of substitutions is substantially lower than in Table 8–1, indicating that the various thresholds are triggered less frequently. While the number of profitable trades remains high, the mean incremental hedge profit from this position is not significantly greater than zero at the 5 percent level for the 25- and 20-basis-point filters. This outcome is due in part to the limited number of observations. With a 15-basis-point threshold, however, the mean incremental hedge profit is 4.8 basis points for the 20 substitutions, which is significant at the 5 percent level.

The results from both tables highlight several additional points. First, the simple trading rule of comparing the TED spread to the cash spread produces a greater number of profitable outcomes than unprofitable outcomes regardless of the filter used. Second, the proportion of favorable outcomes and mean value of the incremental hedge profit declines with less

Table 8-1: Incremental Hedge Profitability of Long Eurodollar or Short T-Bill Futures Substitutions, 1985-1989[a]

Filter	Number of Substitutions (% Profitable)	Incremental Hedge Profit: PRL Min.	Incremental Hedge Profit: PRL Max.	Mean	Profits Mean Per $1 Million Contract	T-test: One-tailed Probability the Mean is ≤ 0	Wilcoxon Z-Value[b]
TED-CSD ≥ 25	44 (54.5%)	-22	50	6.86	$7,700	0.04%	-2.08 (0.019)*
TED-CSD ≥ 20	63 (54.0%)	-31	50	5.05	$7,875	(0.63%)*	-2.25 (0.012)*
TED-CSD ≥ 15	80 (51.3%)	-52	50	2.74	$6,000	(6.69%)	-1.15 (0.125)

* Significant at the 5% level.

a Hedge profits are measured in basis points.

b The figure in parenthesis is the probability of occurrence of the Z-value under the null hypothesis that PRL ≤ 0.

Table 8-2: Incremental Hedge Profitability of Short Eurodollar or Long T-Bill Futures Substitutions, 1985-1989[a]

Filter	Number of Substitutions (% Profitable)	Incremental Hedge Profit: PRL Min.	Max.	Mean	Profits Per $1 Million Contract	T-test: One-tailed Probability the Mean is ≤ 0	Wilcoxon Z-Value[b]
TED-CSD ≤ −25	8 (75.0%)	−15	31	8.50	$1,800	(6.75%)	−1.61 (0.053)
TED-CSD ≤ −20	11 (55.6%)	−15	31	5.36	$1,375	(9.74%)	−1.17 (0.121)
TED-CSD ≤ −15	20 (55.0%)	−13	31	4.80	$2,500	(3.93%)*	−1.85 (0.032)*

* Significant at the 5% level.

a Hedge profits are measured in basis points.

b The figure in parenthesis is the probability of occurrence of the Z-value under the null hypothesis that PRL ≤ 0.

restrictive filters. Finally, in all cases except one, the largest incremental hedge profit exceeded the largest incremental hedge loss by a substantial amount.

While the dollar amount of hedge profits appears to be small for each transaction, the frequency of substitution opportunities makes it worthwhile for a hedger to consider the strategy. For example, results for the 25-basis-point filter in the long Eurodollar substitution indicate that a hedger would have initiated 44 substitutions over the 20 quarters. This allows for just over two substitutions per quarter. The effect of the substitution strategies in the effective yields is additive, so that total profits equal just under 14 basis points per futures contract. This probably represents a sufficient incentive to justify the effort.

III. Summary and Conclusions

This chapter offers a hedge management rule designed to improve hedge performance for traders who want to protect a short-term interest rate exposure. The rule involves identifying instances when three-month Eurodollar futures are relatively expensive or cheap compared to three-month T-bill futures, and selecting the appropriate contract given a hedger's risk exposure. The objective is to enhance hedge profits or diminish hedge losses that would otherwise accrue under traditional hedge practice.

The hedge rule involves comparing the TED spread with the cash spread on comparable three-month Eurodollars and Treasury bills. When substantial differences arise, the two spreads are expected to converge, thereby indicating likely relative price moves. Specifically, when the TED spread exceeds the cash spread, in a steady state environment Eurodollar futures prices would increase in relation to T-bill futures prices. The opposite relative price adjustment would arise when the TED spread is less than the cash spread. Simulations were conducted using data daily from 1985 through 1989 that incorporate substitutions between Eurodollar futures and T-bill futures, based on the simple trading rule. The results indicate that the natural long T-bill hedgers (or the natural short Eurodollar hedgers) would have realized incremental hedge profits in excess of the recommended position by an average of 7 basis points per substitution with the most restrictive filter. Under this tactic, such a hedger would have made substitutions 44 times over the five years, thus allowing for an annualized improvement in yield of approximately 14 basis points. With less restrictive filters the mean incremental hedge profit declined to just over 5 basis points per transaction, but the number of substitutions increased sharply. On an annualized basis, this tactic improved performance by almost 16 basis points. For opposite hedgers (i.e., natural long Eurodollar hedgers and natural short T-bill hedgers) the results were less attractive but still beneficial. Here, the benefit would only have enhanced the outcome by about 5 basis points per annum. The implication is that when both Eurodollar and T-bill futures satisfy the correlation requirements required by hedgers, the use of the simple hedging rule will add value, on average, to the overall hedge outcome.

Despite the rigor that we tried to employ in these tests, three important considerations are not reflected in our analysis. First, the outcomes ignore the impact of transactions costs. Each substitution probably involves selling one futures at its offer price and buying the other futures at its bid price, as well as bearing some commission charges. Thus, an estimated two or three tick "cost" per substitution would represent 8 to 12 basis points annually, which would account for an important portion of any hoped-for gains. The second consideration involves the fact that our rule implies that trades are made only using closing prices. Opportunities that occur in the course of the day, but are not present at the end of the day, are not included in our calculations. Whether these substitutions would have been beneficial or detrimental is uncertain. Finally, and perhaps most significant, is that regardless of the specific results, it may be unrealistic to expect hedgers to apply such a mechanical rule in the real world. In particular, the rules offered herein are based on the assumption that underlying cash Treasury bill and Eurodollar rates will not move differentially to any substantive degree. Certainly, if this expectation were adopted, the application of one of the suggested rules would be both appealing and appropriate. If a hedger had reason to expect non-similar price moves, implementing the rule might be ill-advised.

While our results suggest that some marginal benefit can be realized by managing hedges using rigid decision rules, some caution is also advised. Most mechanical trading rules have their rationale based on underlying assumptions about the way the world works, and therefore implementing such a rule would probably work best when the underlying assumptions are "validated." The results of this paper show statistically significant—albeit limited—profit opportunities for an indiscriminate use of various substitution rules. It offers some promise of more meaningful results if the hedger were more selective about when to implement this type of substitution strategy.

This material is forthcoming in *Financial Analysts Journal*. Permission granted by Financial Analysts Federation, 1992.

The authors would like to thank Joseph Farinella for providing computer assistance.

Endnotes

1   The TED spread convergence will not be perfect or complete because the T-bill and Eurodollar contracts do not expire simultaneously.

2   Such parallel rate movements are not consistent with parallel moves of the two effective rates underlying each instrument.

3   The use of daily closing rates understates the frequency of substitution opportunities, but provides a meaningful measure of value enhancing trades.

4   The Wilcoxon test, unlike the t-test, does not assume that incremental hedge profits are normally and independently distributed.

5   The coefficient of variation for profit measured as the mean profit divided by the standard deviation is virtually the same for all filters.

References

Eaker, M. and D. Grant, "Currency Hedging Strategies for Internationally Diversified Equity Portfolios." *The Journal of Portfolio Management* (Fall 1990) 30-32.

MacDonald, S., Peterson, R., and T. Koch. "Using Futures to Improve Treasury Bill Portfolio Performance." *The Journal of Futures* (April 1988) 167-184.

Chapter

9

Cash-and-Carry Trading and the Pricing of Treasury Bill Futures

(with Timothy W. Koch)

Consiterable effort has been devoted to examining whether the Treasury bill futures market is efficient. Most studies have compared futures yields to coincident forward yields implied by the term-structure of spot market bills, and many have found that numerous arbitrage possibilities are available. The existence of statistically significant differences has been attributed to market inefficiency whenever the differences could not be explained, but numerous explanations have been offered.

Early research focused on the impact of differential transactions costs (Poole 1978, Rendleman & Carrabini 1979), daily settlement for futures trades (Morgan 1978), differential tax influences (Arak 1980), and the cost of guaranteeing performance in futures trades (Kane 1980). More recently, Chow and Brophy (1982) have argued that futures contracts incorporate a differential "habitat premium" that reflects investors' preferences for the more speculative futures transactions. Regardless of the presumed causal factors incorporated in their analyses, many researchers have concluded that arbitrage opportunities have consistently been available over time.

An entirely different focus on the futures-forward yield relationship was provided by Vignola and Dale (1980). They used Working's theory of storage costs to evaluate the impact of financing costs in establishing equilibrium futures prices under pure arbitrage conditions.[1] Working (1949) originally examined commodity prices and argued that the difference between cash and futures prices could be attributed to carrying charges, including transportation, insurance, and warehouse costs, as well as interest. Vignola and Dale applied Working's analysis to Treasury bill futures by comparing actual futures prices to equilibrium futures prices constructed under the assumption that arbitragers borrow the deliverable bills when trading futures. They concluded that carrying costs provide a better explanation of futures prices than unbiased expectations and the term-structure.

This study extends recent research concerning the role of carrying costs and Treasury bill futures. In particular, we examine the pricing of nearby Treasury bill futures with regard to pure arbitrage. Variations in the differential between rates on nearby futures contracts and corresponding forward rates are explained in terms of the spread between rates on term and overnight repurchase agreements. The futures to forward differential, which is typically associated with futures market efficiency, reflects trading strategies employed primarily by U.S. government securities dealers. The arbitrage that drives these rates, the cash-and-carry trade, involves comparing a holding period yield with a financing rate. Traders buy a deliverable Treasury bill and short the corresponding futures contract whenever the yield realized from purchasing the bill, holding it to delivery, and ultimately surrendering the bill in fulfillment of the short contract exceeds their financing cost. Conversely, they borrow the deliverable bill via a reverse repurchase agreement, sell it, and go long the futures contract whenever the holding period yield is less than the financing cost.[2]

Although the decision rule appears to be straightforward, a variety of financing alternatives reflecting various repurchase agreements (RPs) leads to different trading decisions. It is the purpose of this chapter to discuss the different approaches to financing the cash-and-carry trade and to demonstrate that prices on nearby Treasury bill futures are set at the margin via this arbitrage. The analysis helps explain much of the seemingly inefficient behavior in the nearby futures markets described in earlier research.

The remainder of the chapter is structured as follows. The first section describes the arbitrage in more detail and explains why the futures-forward rate differential varies over time. The second section uses daily data to test whether the differential can be explained in terms of speculative arbitrage, and the final section summarizes the results and compares the conclusions with previous studies.

I. Nearby Futures Arbitrage

Market efficiency suggests that traders arbitrage away any differences between the forward rate implied by two spot Treasury bills of different maturities and the futures rate. Inequalities suggest the possibility of arbitrage opportunities. Most studies have thus tested for efficiency by constructing forward rates from yield curve data and comparing these rates with coincident futures rates via mean difference t-tests. While we accept the theoretical soundness of the approach, the arbitrage implied by the futures-forward rate comparison is not the predominant one in the marketplace. The calculation of forward rates focuses on the period beginning with the futures' delivery date and ending 91 days forward. Instead, professional traders and government securities dealers focus on the period from the present to the delivery date of the nearby futures contract and compare a holding period yield with a financing rate.[3]

Consider the following time chart (Figure 9–1). The time line identifies the current date ($t = 0$), the delivery date of the Treasury bill futures contract T days from the present, and the maturity date of the cash bill that matures 91 days following the

Figure 9–1: Time Chart

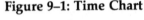

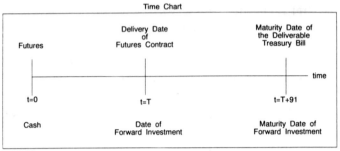

delivery date, T + 91 days from the present. Let R represent the discount rate per \$100 of face value and the notations T and $T91$ refer to the underlying instrument with maturity of T and T + 91 days from the present. The forward rate (RFOR) on a 91-day contract to begin T days from the present is calculated from the following equation:[4]

$$[1-RFOR(91/360)]=[1-RT91(T+91)/360]/[1-RT(T/360)] \quad (1)$$

It is normally argued that if the futures and spot markets are in equilibrium and no inefficiencies exist, the futures rate (RFUT) would equal the forward rate from eq. (1) after adjusting for transaction costs. This comparison suggests that traders focus on 91-day returns available T days from the present. In fact, the true focus of active bill traders covers the interval from the present until the delivery of the nearby futures contract. For example, a trader can effectively lock in a return by purchasing a cash bill with T + 91 days to maturity and simultaneously shorting the nearby futures, thus fixing the selling price of the cash bill T days after purchase. This rate of return (RT*) is commonly referred to as the "implied RP rate" and is calculated on a discount basis from eq. (2):[5]

$$[1-RT^*(T/360)]=[1-RT91(T+91)/360]/[1-RFUT(91/360)] \quad (2)$$

Traders compare the implied RP rate with a financing rate that is typically the actual RP rate available when Treasury securities are used as collateral in a repurchase agreement. Whenever the implied RP rate exceeds the actual RP rate, traders buy the deliverable bill and short the futures as characterized above. Whenever the actual RP rate exceeds the implied RP rate, traders reverse the transactions by borrowing the deliverable bill via a reverse repurchase agreement, selling it, and going long the nearby futures contract. At delivery, the deliverable Treasury bill is immediately returned to its lender, thereby satisfying the reverse repurchase agreement. In either case, any realized difference in the RP rates—implied versus actual—offers a profit opportunity to arbitragers.

With this arbitrage, the futures price is determined at the margin by speculative activity during the three months prior to delivery. Traders buy or sell Treasury bill futures depending on the sign and magnitude of the differential between the implied RP rate and the expected financing rate. Traditional tests of efficiency using forward rates ignore this speculative activity. Instead, it is inferred that futures prices are set relative to 91-day returns available at delivery of the futures contract. It should be noted, however, that the near-term arbitrage is not entirely risk-free. For example, suppose a trader buys a bill with a six-month remaining life and simultaneously sells a three-month futures with a delivery date three months forward. If interest rates on both the cash and futures bill were to fall by 100 basis points, two things would happen: (1) a variation margin payment would be required of $2,500 per futures contract and (2) the cash bill would appreciate in value by $5,000. The two-to-one difference reflects a six-month maturity on the cash bill versus a three-month maturity on the futures. The added collateral value on the cash instrument, however, might not be realized by the cash-and-carry trader, as the bill has been used in a term RP agreement and it was not in the possession of the trader. The trader must then find additional financing to cover the margin call.

If, alternatively, rates increased by 100 basis points, the trader would receive $2,500 for each futures contract, but *might* be required to add $5,000 of collateral to the RP contract. Whether additional financing is required depends upon the margining practice with the RP contract. As these contracts are principal-to-principal agreements, they may be written in a variety of ways. Some allow for marking the collateral to market on a periodic basis as frequently as daily. For others, the terms require only one-way margining. When the value of the bills declines, additional collateral is required, but when a bill appreciates, no "excess collateral" is remitted to the "borrower." When financing overnight, the asymmetrical valuation effects between the cash bill and the futures can be managed by ratio hedging; that is, by adjusting the ratio of cash bills to futures, the cash-flow asymmetries can be minimized.[6]

An important element of the arbitrage, therefore, is the time for which financing is arranged. If traders finance the transactions to the delivery date using a term RP, they eliminate the risk that borrowing costs might increase over the life of the arbitrage, but they bear the risk of additional costs for financing margin calls. If they finance on a shorter-term basis, they are effectively speculating on future movements in RP rates; however, this strategy may permit better management of cash flow requirements.

When testing for market efficiency, the standard comparison of futures to forward rates is equivalent to a comparison of the implied RP rate with the term RP rate. Our fundamental proposition, however, is that the futures-forward rate differential largely reflects traders' practices of financing cash positions on an overnight basis as opposed to any market inefficiencies. In essence, the nearby futures price varies with the overnight RP rate. We hypothesize that whenever the term RP rate is greater (less) than the overnight RP rate (RON), the futures-forward rate differential is positive (negative) with the magnitudes directly related.[7]

In addition, the relationship between the two differentials is likely to be time dependent. The further away delivery is at the initiation of the contracts, the greater is the risk that overnight RP rates will vary prior to delivery—and the wider spread it takes between RP rates to induce traders to speculate.

II. Empirical Evidence

The empirical analysis consists of an examination of the relationships between actual Treasury bill futures rates and forward rates constructed using different assumed financing rates in the arbitrage. The forward rates reflect either assumed term financing or overnight financing. First, we duplicate previous work by testing for the equality of nearby futures rates and corresponding forward rates from Eq. (1) calculated from the term-structure of Treasury yields. This is equivalent to testing whether term RP finance can explain the difference in futures and forward rates. We then construct adjusted forward rates (RFOR*) by substituting the compounded value of the overnight RP rate (RON*) for RT in Eq. (1) such that

$$[1-RFOR^*(91/360)]=[1-RT91(T+91)/360]/(1-RON^*(T/360)) \quad (3)$$

and we retest for equality between RFUT and RFOR*.[8] RFOR* represents the forward rate that is consistent with overnight financing of securities dealers' arbitrage. A zero difference provides evidence that the futures contract is priced according to the cash-and-carry arbitrage. In every instance we segment the analysis in terms of the number of days prior to delivery of the nearby futures contract.

The data employed are daily closing quotations for spot and futures rates from September 1977 through June 1982. This period covers 18 different cash/futures combinations. Futures rates are based on closing settlement prices from the *Daily Information Bulletin* provided by the International Monetary Market. Rates on outstanding Treasury bills and repurchase agreements are offered rates provided by the Bank of America via Data Resources, Inc. The calculations of RFOR and RFOR* reflect the practice of next-day settlement for Treasury bills, so that the daily quoted rate actually applies to the following day's transactions.

Table 9–1 presents the results of the mean difference *t*-tests. Initially, we analyze the arithmetic differences between futures rates on nearby contracts and the associated forward rates calcu-

Table 9–1:
Summary Statistics for Arithmetic Differences:
Futures Rates Minus Forward Rates Calculated
from EQ. (1): Daily Data for September 1977
through June 1982[a]

Statistic	Number of Days to Delivery of Futures Contract					
	Entire Sample	<15	15-29	30-44	45-59	>60
Mean	–0.314	0.006	–0.166	–0.330	–0.434	–0.484
Standard Deviation	0.365	0.232	0.288	0.296	0.316	0.387
Number of Observations	1126	189	191	194	207	345
t-value	–28.8[b]	–0.3	–8.0[b]	–15.5[b]	–19.8[b]	–23.2[b]

a All variables are measured in percentages.
b Significantly different from zero at the 1% level.

lated from Eq. (1). Summary statistics are provided in the top part of Table 9–1, where the *t*-values reported reflect the hypothesis that the futures rate equals the forward rate. The first column presents the results for the entire sample. The other five columns report similar results for the sample segmented according to the number of days to delivery. Interestingly, the mean difference is zero nearest to delivery, becomes negative after 14 days, and grows increasingly larger in absolute terms farther from delivery. The negative means are not surprising given the inverted yield curve that existed over most of the sample period. During that time, overnight RP rates typically exceeded term RP rates so that futures rates were lower than the forward rates inherent in the term-structure. These results would seem to support earlier work that indicated some evidence of market inefficiency.

Similar data are presented in Table 9–2, except that the forward rate (RFOR*) used in the comparison is calculated by substituting the compounded overnight RP rate for RT in Eq. (1). In effect, we are examining whether the futures rate is determined by RON* as traders generally finance their positions on a continuous overnight basis. If this is the case, the computed differential between RFUT and RFOR* should be much smaller than the differential between RFUT and RFOR. In fact, in all cases the mean differences are much smaller when the overnight RP rate is used than they are when the term RP rate is used. Moreover, the contention of market efficiency generally is supported by the data. The mean rate differential is not significantly different from zero over the entire sample period, but significant differences do appear when data are restricted to less than 30 days prior to the delivery day of the futures contract. These differences may be due to the time difference between the collection of the cash market rate and the future market rate on any given day (roughly 1½ hours). With compounding, such a temporal difference may be more important near the delivery date and less so as the delivery day extends into the future.

Table 9–2:
Summary Statistics for Arithmetic Differences:
Futures Rates Minus Forward Rates Calculated
Using the Compounded Overnight RP Rate: Daily
Data for September 1977 through June 1982[a]

Statistic	Entire Sample	<15	15-29	30-44	45-59	>60
			Number of Days to Delivery of Futures Contract			
Mean	−0.030	0.054	0.044	0.013	−0.001	0.037
Standard Deviation	0.479	0.212	0.223	0.287	0.309	0.771
Number of Observations	1126	189	191	194	207	345
t-value	2.1	3.5[b]	2.7[b]	0.6	−0.1	0.9

a All variables are measured in percentages.
b Significantly different from zero at the 1% level.

Importantly, when the sample was restricted to the period from January 1980 to June 1982, a period when Federal Reserve policy targeted bank reserves and permitted greater interest rate volatility than previously, our results were stronger. As demonstrated in Table 9–3, the mean differences were not significantly different from zero for the entire sample, as well as for each of the time intervals prior to delivery.[9] The results further suggest that one need not appeal to such considerations as transaction costs, variation margin uncertainty, tax treatment, and so on, in order to explain futures prices.[10]

The importance of these results is magnified by recent changes in delivery dates for Treasury bill futures. Except on rare occasions prior to the March 1983 contract, arbitrage oppor-

Table 9–3:
Summary Statistics for Arithmetic Differences: Futures Rates Minus Forward Rates Calculated Using the Overnight RP Rate: Daily Data for September 1980 through June 1982[a]

	Number of Days to Delivery of Futures Contract					
Statistic	Entire Sample	<15	15-29	30-44	45-59	>60
Mean	0.041	0.072	0.037	–0.027	0.028	0.072
Standard Deviation	0.640	0.288	0.271	0.351	0.379	1.053
Number of Observations	588	100	101	100	109	178
t-value	1.6	2.5	1.4	–0.8	0.8	0.9

a All variables are measured in percentages.
b Significantly different from zero at the 1% level.

tunities for specific cash/futures combinations were only available for about 90 days, with a cash market instrument that declined in maturity from, at most, 183 days and the nearby futures contract. Beginning June 1983, the Treasury bill delivery cycle was altered so that any original one-year bill could satisfy delivery requirements. Thus the cash-and-carry arbitrage can potentially be extended to nine months. It seems likely that corresponding futures rates on these contracts will come under a greater discipline reflecting this new arbitrage opportunity. Previous studies that have shown significant differences in futures and forward rates on contracts farther from delivery generally have not recognized that the cash-and-carry trade has not been available.

III. Conclusions

This study examines the cash-and-carry trade employed by U.S. government securities dealers to explain why futures rates on nearby Treasury bill contracts differ from corresponding forward rates implied by the Treasury yield curve. The nearby contract is the only one for which the actual deliverable bill has been available. Mean difference t-tests are used to demonstrate that futures rates are determined largely by overnight carrying costs. Specifically, futures rates calculated on the basis of compounded overnight RP rates do not differ significantly from observed futures rates on nearby contracts. Thus the nearby futures market is efficient. The availability of deliverable bills on more distant futures contracts suggests that corresponding arbitrage activity will foster greater efficiency in these distant-month contracts than has been found by earlier researchers.

This chapter is reprinted from the *Journal of Futures Markets*, vol. 4, no. 2, 115-123. © 1984 by John Wiley & Sons, Inc.

Appreciation is expressed to Robert Klassen for providing computer assistance.

Endnotes

1   In pure arbitrage situations a cash position is financed with borrowed funds. This contrasts with quasi-arbitrage transactions that incorporate securities actually owned. Rendleman and Carrabini (1979) and Vignola and Dale (1980) elaborate on this distinction.

2   We focus on nearby futures contracts and the 91 days prior to delivery because deliverable Treasury bills are always

available in the arbitrage. This provides traders the option to lock in a profit whenever they finance to term. Prior to the June 1983 Treasury bill futures cycle, the arbitrage was not always possible farther from delivery. After June 1983, however, the calendar of delivery dates is adjusted to permit the delivery of previously issued one-year bills with 13 weeks remaining life. Vignola and Dale (1980) examine prices beyond 91 days to delivery and do not address the speculative aspects of this pure arbitrage during the time of their investigation. We do not analyze quasi-arbitrage activities or pricing discrepancies in this study.

3 Vignola and Dale point out that pure arbitrage is especially applicable to these market participants who, at the time of a 1979 CFTC Survey, held 34 percent of all outstanding Treasury bill contracts.

4 For consistency, discount rates are used throughout this chapter even though some rates are typically quoted on a money market basis. We ignore transaction costs and other influences that may alter effective rates.

5 Again, in practice, traders tend to calculate this rate on a money market yield basis, but for simplicity, we have chosen to work with a discount rate construction.

6 For example, taking the six-month cash position against a three-month futures, two futures contracts should be used for each million dollars of cash bills. This ratio will decline as the maturity of the cash bill shortens. Thus the cash-and-carry trade becomes an actively managed hedge, where the risks of asymmetrical cash flow considerations can be minimized.

7 Our analysis implicitly assumes that traders expect overnight RP rates to remain constant to term. This treatment is consistent with other studies, such as Hamburger and Platt (1975), which conclude that investors largely act as if they

expect future short-term interest rates to equal current short-term rates.

8 The compounded overnight RP rate (RON*) is calculated as:

$$RON^* = (360/T)[1-(1-RON/360)^T].$$

9 The results from September 1977 through December 1979 were comparable to those in Table 9–2.

10 Using data from 1976 through 1978, Vignola and Dale (1980) demonstrated that mean price differences between futures prices and similarly constructed forward prices cycled around zero. Their study, in contrast, used the federal funds rate as a proxy for overnight carrying costs. We duplicated their tests for the five contracts that overlapped in our sample and obtained comparable results. Comparing price data, actual December 1977 and March 1978 futures prices exceeded projected prices assuming overnight RP financing by an average of $154 and $22, respectively. For the next three contracts, the actual futures prices were $82, $150, and $151 less than the projected prices. These estimates have the same sign as Vignola and Dale's but differ in magnitude. This reflects significant differences in the Federal funds rate and overnight RP rates during each contract period.

Bibliography

Arak, M. "Taxes, Treasury Bills, and Treasury Bill Futures," Federal Reserve Bank of New York (March 1980).

Capozza, D. and Cornell, B. "Treasury Bill Pricing in the Spot and Futures Market," *Review of Economics and Statistics* (November 1979).

Chow, B. and Brophy, D. "Treasury Bill Futures Market: A Formulation and Interpretation," *The Journal of Futures Markets* (Winter 1982).

Hamburger, M. and Platt, E. "The Expectations Hypothesis and the Efficiency of the Treasury Bill Market," *The Review of Economics and Statistics* (May 1975).

Kane, E. "Market-Incompleteness and Divergences Between Forward and Future Interest Rates," *Journal of Finance* (May 1980).

Lang, R. and Rasche, R. "A Comparison of Yields on Futures Contracts and Implied Forward Rates," *Federal Reserve Bank of St. Louis Review* (December 1978).

Morgan, G. "Pricing Treasury Bill Futures Contracts," Comptroller of the Currency (June 1978).

Poole, W. "Using T-Bill Futures to Gauge Interest-Rate Expectations," *Federal Reserve Bank of San Francisco Economic Review* (Spring 1978).

Rendleman, R. and Carrabini, C. "The Efficiency of the Treasury Bill Futures Market," *Journal of Finance* (September 1979).

Vignola, A. and Dale, C. "The Efficiency of the Treasury Bill Futures Market: An Analysis of Alternative Specifications," *Journal of Financial Research* (Fall 1980).

Working, H. "The Theory of Price of Storage," *American Economic Review* (December 1949).

Chapter

10

Yield Opportunities and Hedge Ratio Considerations with Fixed Income Cash-and-Carry Trades

(with Timothy W. Koch)

P rices of nearby futures contracts on fixed-income securities are determined by an arbitrage activity commonly called the cash-and-carry trade. With this trade, an arbitrageur buys or sells the deliverable spot instrument, takes the opposite position with a nearby futures contract, and compares the resulting rate on this synthetic instrument with the prevailing Treasury bill repo rate (or reverse repo rate). If the difference is sufficiently large, the arbitrageur borrows at the lower rate and invests at the higher rate.

Under certain yield conditions, the cash-and-carry trade offers an opportunity that enhances potential returns. Whether the opportunity exists, however, depends on the arbitrageur's hedging objective which, in turn, determines the appropriate hedge ratio. Those who want to equate daily changes of values due to changing interest rates use a hedge ratio that exceeds the hedge ratio used by an arbitrageur who attempts to equate changes in values over longer periods. The first foregoes any yield enhancement opportunity while the second retains it.

This chapter demonstrates the nature of yield opportunities in cash-and-carry trades involving T-bills and explores implications regarding the choice of the appropriate hedge ratio. The fundamental conclusion is that the appropriate hedge ratio depends on the choice of the hedge value date and on the maturity of the instrument being hedged. Yield enhancement opportunities exist only when arbitrageurs finance their positions overnight or for any maturity less than term and use hedge ratios based on the futures delivery date. The first section describes the cash-and-carry trade with T-bills and explains characteristics of the opportunity more fully. The second section examines the choice of hedge ratio and its implications. Important results are summarized in the final section.

Yield Opportunities in Treasury Bill Cash-and-Carry Trades

It is generally recognized that prices on nearby T-bill futures contracts reflect cash-and-carry trading activity (Kawaller and Koch 1984, Gendreau 1985, and Allen and Thurston 1988). Here an arbitrageur identifies the appropriate deliverable security or the optimal spot market instrument that meets the futures contract specifications upon expiration. The purchase of this particular security coupled with the simultaneous sale of the futures contract synthetically shortens the maturity of the deliverable instrument and establishes a holding period yield over the time horizon from the value date of the purchase to the futures delivery date. This yield, designated the implied repo rate, is then compared to the prevailing repo rate in the spot market. When the implied repo rate exceeds the actual repo rate, arbitrageurs will borrow at the prevailing repo rate, buy the deliverable bill, and sell the futures contract to yield the implied repo rate. The net return equals the implied repo rate less transactions and financing costs. Alternatively, when the actual repo rate exceeds the implied repo rate, arbitrageurs will borrow by selling the deliverable bill, buy the futures contract, then invest via a reverse repo transaction. The net return here equals the effective term repo rate minus the implied repo rate net of transactions cost.

Chapter Nine demonstrated that for Treasury bills the implied repo rate equaled the actual repo rate, on average, from 1977 to 1982 due to arbitrage activity. For Treasury bonds, in contrast, the implied repo rate has been shown to be consistently below the prevailing repo rate (Klemkosky and Lasser 1985, Kolb, Gay, and Jordan 1982, and Resnick and Hennigar 1983). Most of the studies attribute the difference to the fact that sellers of Treasury bond futures have a choice of which long-term security to deliver at expiration, along with several timing choices as to when to deliver. Because these delivery choices have value and favor the short futures position, the futures price is depressed relative to what it would be if no delivery choices existed. [1]

The nature of the yield opportunity in the cash-and-carry trade can be demonstrated by analyzing the specific features of a traditional transaction involving three-month T-bill futures. An arbitrageur identifies the currently traded cash Treasury bill that will have three months remaining maturity at the first delivery day of the futures contract. This security currently has a maturity greater than three months. The traditional arbitrage consists of buying the cash bill and simultaneously selling futures to establish an implied repo rate for a holding period from the present to the first delivery day of the Treasury bill futures contract.

Assume a spot value date of April 1 and a nearby futures delivery date of June 23. On April 1, the deliverable cash Treasury bill has a 174-day maturity, segmented as 83 days remaining to delivery plus 91 days from delivery until maturity on September 24. The purchase price of the deliverable bill (Pb) is determined by the traditional formula;

$$P_b = \text{Par}[1 - R(d/360)] \qquad (1)$$

where Par equals the par value of the Treasury bill at maturity, R is the discount rate, and d is the number of days to maturity.

With a $1 million par value and a discount rate on the deliverable bill of 6.50 percent, the invoice price determined by substituting the appropriate values in equation (1) is $968,583.33.

The sale of a June futures contract establishes a projected price at delivery, also determined by equation (1), but with the futures discount rate substituted for the cash rate and only 91 days to maturity. Assuming a futures rate of 6.40 percent, the projected futures invoice price is $983,822.22. The implied repo rate thus equals the projected futures price minus the purchase invoice price expressed as an annualized money market rate. In this example, the 83-day holding period yield, or implied repo rate, is determined as a money market rate, as follows:

$$\text{Implied repo rate} = \left[\frac{\$983,822.22 - \$968,583.33}{968,583.33}\right] \times \left[\frac{360}{83}\right] = 6.824\%$$

An arbitrageur will earn this precise implied repo rate only if the futures and cash rates equal 6.40 percent at expiration of the futures contract. Slight discrepancies usually occur because rates vary between the initial transactions and expiration. Table 10–1 demonstrates the potential magnitude of these discrepancies when rates alternatively fall and rise.

Consider a decline in the June futures and cash rate to 4.40 percent at delivery (column 1). With lower rates, the futures position produces a cumulative loss of $5,000, equal to $25 for each basis point times the 2 percent change in rates. The cash Treasury bill, in contrast, increases by $5,055.56 over its initial projected value to $988,877.78 as each basis point is valued at $25.28.[2] The difference reflects the fact that the cash Treasury bill has 91 days remaining to maturity rather than 90 days assumed in futures pricing. Thus the unanticipated gain on the cash position exceeds the loss on the futures position by $55.56, thereby improving the realized return to 6.849 percent.

The data in column 3 similarly demonstrate the effect of an increase in rates on the realized return from this series of transactions. With rising rates, the futures position increases in value, but the $5,000 gain is less than the $5,055.56 decline in the value of the cash bill below its projected value. The realized return thus drops to 6.799 percent.[3]

The implication of Table 10–1 is simply that the implied repo rate is largely insensitive to changes in the general level of interest rates, so that traders can anticipate the outcome of their position with a high degree of reliability. This assumes, however, that arbitrageurs finance their positions to term or use term reverse RPs. If instead they use overnight RPs or any maturity instrument less than term, the net return from the trade may vary from that expected. Specifically, the realized profit will decline when rates rise above what is expected and will rise

Table 10–1:
The Effect of Interest Rate Changes on the
Realized Return to the Cash-and-Carry Trade

	Interest Rate Changes after the Initial Transaction		
	1. Lower Rates	2. No Change in Rates	3. Higher Rates
Settlement rate	4.40%	6.40%	8.40%
Settlement price	$988,877.78	$983,822.22	$978,766.67
Purchase price	968,583.33	968,583.33	968,583.33
Gain on cash	20,294.44	15,238.89	10,183.34
Final futures price	95.60	93.60	91.60
Futures profit/loss	–5,000.00	0.00	5,000.00
Net gain on combined position	15,294.44	15,238.89	15,183.34
Return on investment	6.849%	6.824%	6.799%

when rates fall below what is expected with the traditional cash-and-carry trade. The opposite relationship holds for the reverse cash-and-carry trade combination.

Yield Enhancement Through Early Unwinding

Results prescribed in Chapter Nine support the use of overnight financing or overnight reverse *RP* investing. Allen and Thurston's (1988) results, on the other hand, are more consistent with transactions to term. Only in the case of overnight or less-than-term transactions, however, can arbitrageurs enhance yields from the cash-and-carry trade through early unwinding.

The yield enhancement opportunity in a cash-and-carry trade derives from the difference between the change in values of the deliverable Treasury bill and the futures position. This difference becomes exaggerated during the period prior to the futures expiration. Whenever interest rates decline, after the implementation of the traditional cash-and-carry trade, an arbitrageur may have the opportunity to liquidate the combined positions prior to futures expiration and earn a substantially higher rate of return, albeit for a shorter holding period.[4] When interest rates increase, the arbitrageur can hold the position to futures expiration and earn the implied repo rate, plus or minus the several-basis-point discrepancy per Table 10–1. In this case, however, the arbitrageur faces higher financing costs. Implicitly, the initial rate discrepancy between implied repo and actual repo rates should cover the *effective* term repo rate expected, even if overnight financing is used. If rates increase more than originally expected, profit declines. The opposite holds with the reverse cash-and-carry trade.

Ignoring the financing uncertainties, consider, for example, how the previous cash-and-carry trade changes in value if cash and futures rates change sharply within the course of a day. The first column in Table 10–2 demonstrates that an arbitrageur realizes an annualized overnight return of almost 50 percent if both

Table 10–2:
The Effect of Overnight Interest Rate Changes on the
Realized Return to the Cash-and-Carry Trade

	1. Lower Rates	2. Higher Rates
Initial days to maturity	174 days	174 days
Initial discount rate	6.500%	6.500%
Initial invoice price	$968,583.33	$968,583.33
Next-day's days to maturity	173 days	173 days
Next-day's discount rate	6.000%	7.000%
Next-day's invoice price	971,166.67	966,361.11
Change in invoice value	2,583.33	–2,222.22
Initial futures price	93.60	93.60
Next-day's futures price	94.10	93.10
Profit/loss on futures	–1,250.00	1,250.00
Consolidated profit/loss	1,333.33	–972.22
Overnight R.O.I. (annual rate)	49.557%	–36.135%

cash and futures rates fall by 50 basis points the day after the cash-and-carry trade is implemented.

$$\text{Realized return} = \left[\frac{\$1,333.33}{\$968,583.33}\right] \times \left[\frac{360}{1}\right] = 49.557\%$$

Because the deliverable Treasury bill has 173 days to maturity and not the 90 days assumed in futures pricing, the bill's value increases by $2,583.33 while the loss on the futures position (increase in futures variation margin) totals just $1,250. If such a liquidation were effected, additional financing charges would not be realized. Thus the arbitrageur could liquidate the combined position and earn $1,333.33 overnight.

The second column in Table 10–2 shows that an increase in rates produces the opposite result. Specifically, a 50-basis-point jump in rates generates a consolidated loss of $972.22 if the position is liquidated.[5] Instead, the cash-and-carry trader would hold this position until either rates drop back down or futures expire. Still, the trader might need additional collateral if the deliverable Treasury bill is used as a self-financing vehicle, because the decline in value exceeds the gain from the futures position.[6]

This yield opportunity exists for both the direct cash-and-carry trade described above and the reverse, wherein an arbitrageur sells the deliverable Treasury bill and buys futures. A reverse is justified whenever the actual repo rate exceeds the implied repo rate. Constructing a reverse cash-and-carry trade effectively creates a liability or borrowing facility. Whenever the positions are held to maturity, the realized term financing rate will equal the initial implied repo rate plus or minus the small adjustment for rate changes, similar to that in Table 10–1. In contrast with the traditional cash-and-carry trade, however, the reverse carries a yield enhancement opportunity that increases in value when interest rates rise. Higher rates potentially lower the effective borrowing rate when the gain on the deliverable bill exceeds the loss on futures, though the financing period is shortened. The fact that the yield opportunity applies equally for direct and reverse cash-and-carry trades suggests that it exerts a price-neutral effect on futures prices.

Although these examples use Treasury bills, the same opportunities exist with virtually any commodity for which a cash-and-carry trade can be constructed. Occasionally, however, there are complications. In the case of Treasury bonds and notes, for example, implementing a cash-and-carry trade is complicated by the conversion factor system in pricing futures and determining the deliverable bond. Brennan and Schwartz (1987) explain a similar position for stock index futures arbitrage. In this case, however, perturbations that foster price shifts in stock index hedging and arbitrage tend to produce changes of roughly equivalent values for the underlying stocks and futures contracts. This suggests that the value of the timing opportunity should be substantially smaller for stock index/futures arbitrage versus that for fixed-income/futures arbitrage. Moreover, within the realm of fixed-income arbitrage, the most pronounced opportunities will exist for short-term instruments. This is because the passage of time creates a greater change in the value of a basis point when the time in question represents a "significant" share of the maturity of the security. For example, 15 days hardly affect the value of a basis point on a 10-year bond but they dramatically change the value of a basis point on a three-month bill.

The Choice of Hedge Ratio

Profit opportunities with the cash-and-carry trade vary with the objectives and strategies of each arbitrageur. If a position is financed on an overnight basis, the trade offers a yield opportunity to the arbitrageur. If financed to term, no such opportunity exists. Similarly, the correct hedge ratio is determined by the remaining maturity of the deliverable bill *at delivery*. Thus, even if the current maturity of the bill is 174 days when the arbitrage is initiated, the appropriate hedge ratio is one futures contract for each $1 million par amount.

This hedge ratio is determined by comparing the value of a basis point associated with the deliverable Treasury bill upon the delivery date to the value of a basis point ($25) on a Treasury bill futures contract.[7] In general, that is, for nondelivery date circumstances, the value of a basis point (V) can be determined from:

$$V = Par\,(.0001)\left[\frac{d}{360}\right] \qquad (2)$$

where d equals the number of days until maturity. The one-to-one hedge ratio assumed earlier was obtained by dividing a basis point value of $25.28 for the cash Treasury bill by $25, but this ratio would clearly exceed unity for Treasury bills with maturity beyond three months.[8] Suppose, for example, that the objective is to hedge the overnight exposure of the same deliverable Treasury bill rather than the exposure until the futures expiration. Implicitly, the goal is to equate changes in cash and futures values on a daily basis. To achieve this end, the hedge ratio should reflect the next day's maturity. Hedging interest rate risk in the previous example now requires calculating the revised value of a basis point as the original Treasury bill changes from a 174-day to a 173-day instrument. In this case, the value of a basis point for the cash bill equals $48.06, and the appropriate hedge ratio becomes 1.92 futures contracts per $1 million of par value bills.[9]

As structured, the hedge ratio necessarily decreases as time passes, until it reaches unity at delivery. Thus a trader who wants to hedge changes in values on a daily basis must continuously rebalance the hedge. Toevs and Jacob (1986) essentially make this same point by distinguishing between "strong form" and "weak form" hedges. In general, a trader who chooses to hedge to value date other than delivery day uses a different hedge ratio determined by the targeted value date.

Features of Value-Equating Hedges

Such value-equating hedges have several unattractive features. Hedge traders using this type of hedge forego the yield enhancement opportunity inherent in the traditional cash-and-carry trade because changes in cash values due to interest rate changes are exactly offset by changes in futures values. Also, the hedge does not take into account price changes in the cash Treasury bill due solely to the passage of time and the natural accretion of price to par. Thus, a hedger might still realize substantial losses on the combined position.

Consider a government securities dealer who decides to hedge a deliverable bill that has a current maturity of 180-days.

The appropriate value-equating hedge requires two futures contracts per $1 million dollars par. The value of the basis point on the cash bill is $50 vs. $25 for the futures. Over the next three months, assuming away rounding problems, the hedge ratio will be reduced systematically to unity by the delivery day, due to the declining maturity and declining value of a basis point. Assume that immediately after initiating the hedge, interest rates rise by X basis points and remain at the higher level until the final hedge ratio adjustment. Then, when the actual hedge ratio is one-to-one, rates fall by the same X basis points. In this case, the interest rate induced price effect on the cash market instrument is zero, given that the initial rate change ultimately is reversed. In contrast, the consolidated hedge profits are nonzero. When rates rose, twice as many contracts were maintained as compared to when rates fell. Thus, even though the hedge ratio is designed to equate these changes in cash values with futures profits (losses) on a day-to-day basis, the objective is not likely to be realized over time.

The above situation may not be relevant for a government bill dealer who maintains an inventory of bills to service customer orders and wants to eliminate interest rate exposure. Here the hope is to profit solely from high turnover whereby the dealer can earn the bid-ask spread. Clearly, hedging with a value date that corresponds to the futures delivery date would be inappropriate since the cash market basis point value is not likely to be $25. Hedging with the next-day's value of a basis point as the determining feature may similarly have the undesirable cumulative effects previously described. While no perfect solution exists, a dealer can estimate the average holding period length that defines the relevant hedge value date, and hedge the position to that date. Earlier sales will necessarily mean insufficient hedge coverage and later sales will mean excessive coverage, but if the average is reasonably reliable and if the size of the inventory remains fairly stable, the imbalance should even out over time.

Summary

Cash-and-carry trading links futures prices with cash prices on deliverable securities. Arbitrageurs who finance their positions on an overnight basis or for any period less than term retain a yield enhancement opportunity. For arbitrageurs who buy the deliverable instrument and sell futures, the opportunity arises when interest rates fall. Those that initiate the reverse cash-and-carry trade see this opportunity arise when interest rates rise.

This opportunity is available whenever arbitrageurs employ a hedge ratio determined by targeting the futures delivery date as the specific trade date. It is not available for traders who want to hedge changes in cash and futures values on a daily basis.

This chapter is reprinted from the *Journal of Futures Markets*, Vol. 9, No. 6, 539-545 (1989) © 1989 by John Wiley & Sons, Inc.

We appreciate the helpful comments of Alex Arapoglou of Chemical Bank as well as those of an anonymous reviewer.

Endnotes

1 The difference between the implied repo rate and actual repo rate reflects the value of this delivery option.

2 $1,000,000(.0001)(91/360) = $25.28.

3 Arbitrageurs do not normally view these changes in returns as a significant problem or benefit with the cash-and-carry trade.

4 The owner of any cash Treasury bill has the same option.

5   The table is not meant to suggest that a parallel rate shift is expected. Clearly, the relationship of the two rate moves would depend on whether the basis were normal or inverted and whether rates were rising or falling. For example, with futures rates above spot rates in a declining rate environment, one would expect slightly higher rate moves on the part of the futures. Given the same basis conditions in a rising rate environment, one would expect the opposite ordering.

6   The terms of repurchase agreements may not provide for additional credit extension in response to rising collateral requirements.

7   This assumes that the discount rate on a cash bill moves one-for-one with the associated futures rate.

8   See endnote 2.

9   With Treasury bonds/notes the value of basis point must be calculated for the cheapest to delivery security using the present value formula, multiplied by the conversion factor.

Bibliography

Allen, L., and Thurston, T. "Cash-Futures Arbitrage and Forward-Futures Spreads in the Treasury Bill Market." *Journal of Futures Markets* (October 1988).

Brennan, M., and Schwartz, E. "Arbitrage in Stock Index Futures." Working paper (July 1987).

Gendreau, B. "Carrying Costs and Treasury Bill Futures." *Journal of Portfolio Management* (Fall 1985).

Kawaller, I. and Koch, T. "Cash-and-Carry Trading and the Pricing of Treasury Bill Futures." *Journal of Futures Markets* (Summer 1984).

Klemkosky, R. and Lasser, D. "An Efficiency Analysis of the T-Bond Futures Market." *Journal of Futures Markets* (Winter 1985).

Kolb, R., Gay, G., and Jordan, J. "Are There Arbitrage Opportunities in the Treasury Bond Futures Markets?" *Journal of Futures Markets* (Fall 1982).

Resnick, B. and Hennigar, E. "The Relationship Between Futures and Cash Prices for U.S. Treasury Bonds." *Review of Research in Futures Markets*, vol.2, no.1 (1983).

Toevs, A. and Jacob, D. "Futures and Alternative Hedge Ratio Methodologies." *Journal of Portfolio Management* (Spring 1986).

Part

II

Currencies

Chapter

11

Currency Futures
Arbitrage

The arbitrage between currency futures and the underlying currency markets not only ensures good prices from the futures markets—it may mean better prices. That is, for some foreign exchange traders, the use of futures as an alternative to the interbank forward market may provide a price advantage, and the futures arbitrage is at the root of this opportunity.

Like other futures contracts, the price of any currency futures contract is determined in the appropriate pit at the exchange via the traditional open outcry process; also like all other futures contracts, these futures prices are closely tied to the markets that underlie the contracts—specifically the interbank currency markets. In fact, with currencies, the underlying markets and the futures markets may be more closely tied than in any other case. This is because the interbank market offers an exceptionally liquid forward market, as well as a deep and active spot market. As a consequence, currency futures are arbitraged against both spot and forward interbank currency markets, so that the futures price and the forward price are determined via the same mechanism—that is, "covered interest arbitrage."

Covered interest arbitrage is a process by which one may be able to earn a profit by (a) borrowing dollars, (b) converting those dollars to a foreign currency, (c) making a bank deposit in that currency and thus earning interest in that currency, and (d) converting principal plus interest back to dollars at the common maturity date of the loan and the bank deposit, for the repayment of the loan plus interest. If the repayment of the dollar-based loan leaves any extra dollars, an arbitrage activity exists. If not, the reverse arbitrage (that is borrowing foreign exchange and investing in dollars) may offer a profitable opportunity.

In the economist's jargon, equilibrium exists when interest rates and exchange rates are such that no arbitrage activity is warranted. This condition would exist whenever the following condition held:[1]

$$(1 + R_{US}\frac{d}{360}) = \frac{F}{S}(1 + R_{FOR}\frac{d}{360})$$

where R_{US} = interest rate (in decimals) on the dollar borrowing (or deposit, for the reverse arbitrage)

d = days of loan (deposit) maturity

F = futures price ($/FX)

S = spot price ($/FX)

R_{FOR} = interest rate on foreign exchange deposit (borrowing)

The left side of the equation reflects the principal plus interest on the dollar-based loan, and the right side of the equation reflects the conversion of these dollars to the foreign exchange, the investment, and the reconversion back to dollars of the foreign-based principal plus interest. It should be clear that if the two dollar values are equal, no arbitrage will be performed. From the above equation one can solve for the theoretical value of the futures price, $\hat{F}$, as follows:

$$\hat{F} = S \cdot \frac{(1 + R_{US}\frac{d}{360})}{(1 + R_{FOR}\frac{d}{360})}$$

Many prefer a simpler approximation to this equation and use the following equation:

$$\hat{F} = S(1+(R_{US}-R_{FOR})\frac{d}{360}).$$

This equation highlights the role of the U.S./foreign interest rate differential. If U.S. rates are higher, the futures price will tend to be at a premium to the spot exchange rates, and vice versa. Importantly, all exchange rates are expressed in American terms—that is, dollars per foreign currency.

The equation provides a close approximation to the more precise original, and generally the differences in the calculated values for $\hat{F}$ are considered to be inconsequential. It may be important to note, however, that the approximation breaks down when either the interest rate differential is large or the term of d is great.

For the arbitrageur, the specific interest rates to be used in the calculation should reflect the rates at which dollars could be borrowed and foreign exchange can be invested, or vice versa. In many cases arbitrageurs may be banks that operate as market makers in the interbank deposit markets. Thus euro-currency deposit rates are typically those used in the calculation. Whether bid or offered rates are used in the equation would depend on whether the specific arbitrageur were able to attract funds at the bid side of the deposit market and place them at the offered side (which would be the most attractive conditions). More likely, however, because of the reactive nature of the arbitrage, the arbitrageur would probably be a price taker on at least one side of the market. For this reason most of those who evaluate the theoretical value of the futures contract tend to use either bids *or* offers on both interest rates used in the calculation.[2]

An analogous choice must be made between the bid and the offer on the spot exchange rate. Again, the arbitrageur would use exchange rates in the equation for which he or she could actually purchase or sell the spot currency. It should be clear then that in fact two different theoretical prices would be relevant—one applying to the long spot/short futures opening arbitrage position and the other applying to the short spot/long futures opening trade. One way of dealing with this practical issue is to calculate the futures price based on the middle of the market for the spot exchange rate, and arbitrage only when the actual futures price differs "sufficiently" from this value.

The nature of the currency arbitrage is such that the futures price typically remains quite close to the theoretical value—so close, in fact that arbitrageurs hope to make as little as one or two ticks (perhaps $25) per contract, with each arbitrage trade. The tightness of this arbitrage has a very important implication: The arbitrage activity virtually assures futures market participants that they will trade at the best interbank prices. These prices must be adjusted, however, to reflect the fact that commissions are charged in the futures market while they are not charged in the interbank market. Thus there is a trade-off between a narrow bid/ask spread along with commissions in the futures market, versus a generally wider bid/ask spread (particularly for non-bankers) in the interbank market. It should be clear that a smaller transaction would therefore favor the use of the futures market, while a larger trade would be better served in the interbank market—at least on a simple price basis (i.e., ignoring flexibility, liquidity concerns, ease of access to information, and so on). As a very general rule of thumb, the non-bank hedger or speculator who trades less than $1 or $2 million per trade probably trades in the futures market at a more attractive all-inclusive price than that available in the interbank market. For this trader the futures market may be considered to be a wholesale market, while in the interbank market, he would be required to pay retail.

This chapter is reprinted from *Bank Asset/Liability Management*, February 1988 (New York: Warren, Gorham & Lamont) © 1988 Warren, Gorham & Lamont, Inc. Used with permission.

Endnotes

1   If one were evaluating arbitrage opportunities for either British Pound Sterling or Canadian dollars, 365 would be substituted for 360. This difference reflects the convention in the interbank market that assumes a 365-day year for these two currencies and a 360-day year for the others.

2   If the bid/offer spread is constant, middle of the market quotes would yield the same interest rate differential.

Chapter

12

Using Futures Contracts to Manage Foreign Exchange Rate Exposure

A ny money manager who has dealt with international currencies over the last several years recognizes that changes in exchange rates can mean considerable adjustments to the bottom line. Sometimes these adjustments are helpful, and sometimes they are not. In either case, many managers view exchange rate-related costs or benefits as random events (i.e., conditions that arise because of external forces far beyond the control of the individual manager). Using currency futures, however, a foreign exchange manager is in a position to control this exposure and substantially mitigate the risks inherent in the international currency markets.

The job of the foreign exchange manager then becomes one of assessing when the risk of adverse exchange rate movements should be taken and when it should be avoided. Essentially, some type of forecasting of exchange rate moves lies at the core of this managerial responsibility. In order to use currency futures, however, one need not make a specific forecast. Instead, one must simply determine whether or not to accept the risk that exchange rates may move adversely. If the probability of an adverse exchange rate move is deemed to be limited and, in fact, a beneficial move seems more likely, the decision to assume the risk (i.e., to remain unhedged) may be appropriate. On the other hand, if an adverse move seems more likely or if it is viewed as desirable to eliminate even the risk of such a move, futures hedging offers a solution.

In general, hedging with currency futures simply involves taking a futures position that will generate profits equal to the losses associated with an adverse spot exchange rate move. A long hedge protects against a rise in a non-U.S. currency value and a short hedge protects against a decline in a non-U.S. A long hedge would be used, say, by a U.S. importer who pays in non-U.S. currencies or perhaps by a borrower who must repay foreign currency. Both have an obligation to make a forthcoming payment with a risk that the non-U.S. currency will become more expensive. In contrast, a short hedge would be used by a U.S. exporter who is paid in non-U.S. currency or a non-U.S. importer who buys goods with U.S. dollars. The short hedge would thus be appropriate when a fixed amount of non-U.S. currency is expected to translate into fewer dollars at some future settlement date.

The next four sections answer the following questions:

1. How many futures contracts should be used for any given hedge?
2. Which contract months should be transacted?
3. What risks are inherent in using futures as a hedge?
4. What degree of uncertainty exists for any expected hedged position?

Number of Futures Contracts

The number of futures contracts needed is determined from a straightforward arithmetic calculation. Consider a situation where a non-U.S. currency must be translated into dollars. Assuming this currency is traded as a futures contract—a necessary condition for any futures hedging strategy—you simply divide the amount of non-U.S. currency by the number of currency units per contract (size of the contract). For example, assume you have to translate one million deutsche marks into dollars. Given 125,000 deutsche marks per contract, eight contracts are needed.

Since contracts specify a fixed number of currency units (i.e., non-U.S. dollars), working with a fixed number of U.S. dollars is slightly more complicated. For example, assume an exposure of $1 million and a futures price of $0.50 per deutsche mark. At that futures price, $1 million would translate into 2 million deutsche marks; and 2 million deutsche marks would be made up of 16 deutsche mark contracts. Note that any hedge will have the effect of fixing the forthcoming exchange rate for the futures value date, only for the number of currency units covered by the futures.

Best Futures Contract Months

The determination of the best futures contract month involves a small amount of discretion. Currency futures contracts are actively traded on a quarterly cycle, with settlement dates on the third Wednesday of March, June, September, and December. The general rule for choosing the "correct" futures contract month is to pick the contract month immediately following the desired date of the actual currency conversion. For example, if you want to make an actual conversion on November 1, the closest futures contract following November is the December contract. However, following the general rule is not always the best practice. Specifically, liquidity considerations may deter the manager from implementing a hedge with a contract that expires too far into the future. As a practical matter, the contracts with the most immediate expirations (the nearby contracts) are traded much more actively than the more distant, or deferred, contracts. Thus, the alternative to initiating a futures trade with a deferred contract is to start by initiating a nearby futures contract; then, as the nearby contract's delivery date approaches, the manager liquidates that position and initiates a new position in a subsequent contract month, and so forth, until the hedge is no longer required.[1] This approach to hedging, called stacking and rolling, may be more reasonable if the hedge manager wants to maintain the ability to eliminate a distant hedge position well before the originally intended hedge date. Such a decision might become appropriate if economic conditions change, making beneficial exchange rate moves more likely. With less liquidity in the more distant months, liquidating the hedge might be costly because the order to liquidate could conceivably move the price on the deferred futures.

Risks Inherent in Hedging with Futures

After deciding how many contracts to use and in which months to place the contract order, three risks need to be considered. The first risk has to do with variation margin and cash-flow uncertainty. All futures contracts are marked-to-market, with profits and losses settled daily. That is, as contract prices change, losers pay and winners receive, every day. Importantly, winners and losers do not settle with each other directly. Through their brokers, they each settle daily with the exchange clearinghouse, making creditworthiness considerations about the trading partner irrelevant. For example, take the hedger who has to sell deutsche marks for dollars to protect against the risk that the value of deutsche marks will decline (the dollar will strengthen). Assume a position of a single June contract at a price of $0.5000 per deutsche mark. A move of two ticks (each tick is $0.0001) to $0.4498 would change the value of the position by 2 × $12.50, or $25.[2] Thus, because the price declined, the long position would have to pay $25 and the short position would receive this amount. For a price rise, the direction of these cash flows would be reversed. As a practical matter, the timing of such a price move is entirely uncertain, and so is the associated opportunity cost (financing charges) or benefit (potential interest income).

As an extreme case, suppose the exchange rate rises sharply immediately after the short futures position is initiated. The position holder would be required to make a variation margin payment and the true cost of this hedge would have to include the financing for the opportunity cost of this variation margin payment. Clearly, these financing charges would be different if the same price change occurred say, three months later or if the price change occurred gradually over time.

The opposite case might also transpire. That is, exchange rates could decline, generating profits for the short futures position. In this case, the hedge could actually earn money as a result of the hedge profits being deposited in an interest-bearing account. Again, these opportunity profits could vary, depending on whether the price move came immediately after the imposition of the futures position or at some future date. As the prospective time path of exchange rate movements is unknown, the true cost of a hedge cannot be determined in advance.[3]

The second risk—and perhaps this is more a condition to simply be accepted than it is a risk, per se—is called basis risk. As mentioned earlier, because spot and futures exchange rates are different at any point in time (as a result of differential interest rates for dollar-denominated bank deposits versus other currency-denominated deposits and varying lengths of time to delivery), the offset realized from a futures position relative to a change in the value of the spot exchange rate may not be exactly one-to-one. As a rule, the futures exchange rate will be higher than a spot exchange rate whenever appropriate maturity Euro-dollar rates exceed Euro-rates of the other currency, and vice versa.[4] The degree to which the hedge position matches the change of the spot exchange rate will depend on the size of the initial difference between spot and futures exchange rates and direction of the subsequent move in exchange rates. For example, assume a short futures position starting from a premium basis—say, with the futures exchange rate at \$0.5500 and the spot exchange rate at \$0.5400. If this position is held until the futures exchange rate and the spot exchange rate converge, any downward move of the futures exchange rate will exceed a downward move of the spot exchange rate by \$0.01 per currency unit, the amount of the initial basis. On a percentage basis, however, the larger the exchange rate move, the smaller the "overage." On the other hand, with a rise in the exchange rate, the short hedge loss will be smaller than the amount of the rise in the spot exchange rate, again by the size of the starting basis. In this case, a higher percentage hedge offset (although always less than 100 percent) would occur with larger exchange rate increase. The risk that the hedge will "overperform" or "underperform," therefore, will depend on the direction of the exchange rate move and the initial positions of the basis.[5]

The final risk to consider when hedging with currency futures occurs when the stacking and rolling procedure is implemented. This practice results in another potential cost or benefit. When futures positions are liquidated in a given month and reinitiated in a subsequent contract month, the price differential will either enhance the performance of the hedge or detract from it. However, the variation in the spread price is generally stable, barring sharp shifts in the relevant interest rate differential.

The ultimate point of this discussion is that hedging, while being straightforward in concept, has a number of practical aspects that could cause actual performance to be different from expected performance. Generally, hedge managers seek a dollar-for-dollar offset on any change in the exchange rate during a hedge period; but because of uncertain cash flow associated with variation margin receipts and payments, the existence of basis risk, and the possible need to roll hedges in order to cover exposures scheduled beyond the expiration dates of actively traded contracts, the realistic manager must recognize that the perfect hedge is an ideal that is unlikely to be realized. Nonetheless, the crucial choice is whether to hedge and achieve as close an offset as possible or to not hedge and be fully exposed to exchange rate risk.

Figure 12–1 shows hedges for four different cases: a U.S. importer, a non-U.S. exporter, a U.S. exporter, and a non-U.S. importer. In all cases, the hedge is designed to insulate the foreign exchange manager from an adverse change in exchange rates. As the examples show, however, the hedges offer inexact coverage, sometimes exceeding the effect of the spot exchange rate move and sometimes falling a bit short. Moreover, as the last example in Figure 12–1 demonstrates, a futures hedge will also offset a beneficial move in the spot market (i.e., futures may generate losses). As the objective of the hedge is to eliminate risk, however, one must accept the coincident consequence of eliminating opportunity as well.

Assessing Futures Hedging Uncertainty

The hedge manager can assess the likely outcome of a hedge position or possibly the more relevant best case/worst case extremes by generating an array of projected futures prices for combinations of extreme movement of spot rates and interest rate differentials.[6] One can develop confidence in a hedge program by examining four cases: (1) a sharply higher spot exchange rate and a sharply higher interest rate differential; (2) a sharply higher spot exchange rate and a sharply lower interest rate differential; (3) a sharply lower spot exchange rate and a sharply lower interest rate differential; and (4) a sharply lower spot exchange rate and a sharply higher interest rate differential.

This chapter is reprinted from *Futures and Options Hedging Software*, Chicago Mercantile Exchange (Chapter 3), 1988.

Figure 12-1: Four Cases of Futures Hedging—Case I

The Long Futures Hedge—U.S. Firm

In early September, a U.S. importer signs a contract to buy German goods in early December for a total cost of DM125,000.

The risk: The cost of the deutsche mark will rise between early September and early December.

The solution: Buy a December DM futures contract in September. Then, when the currency is needed, purchase DM125,000 in the spot market and liquidate the December DM contract

	At Hedge Initiation	At Hedge Liquidation	Change
Spot ($/FX)	$0.6107	$0.5924	($0.0183)
Spot (FX/$)	DM1.6375	DM1.6881	DM0.0506
Futures ($/FX)	$0.6045	$0.5917	($0.0128)
# Contracts (Long)	1	1	
Spot Exposure (FX units)	DM125,000	DM125,000	0
Spot Exposure ($)	$76,337.50	$74,047.38	$2,290.13
Futures Values ($)	$75,562.50	$73,957.17	($1,605.33)
Net Results of Hedging			
= Futures Result + Change in Spot Exposure =			$684.80

Effective Exchange Rate
$0.6052/DM
DM1.6523/$

Figure 12-1: Four Cases of Futures Hedging—Case II

The Long Futures Hedge—Non-U.S. Firm

In early September, a German exporter signs a contract to sell German goods for $250,000 (U.S.). The settlement day is specified for early December.

The risk: The value of the deutsche mark will rise (the value of the dollar will decline) between early September and early December.

The solution: Buy three December DM futures contracts in September. (Note: Three contracts because $250,000 ÷ ($.6607 × DM125,000) ≈ 3.) Then, when the dollar payment is received, use the $250,000 to buy deutsche marks in the spot market and liquidate the futures position.

	At Hedge Initiation	At Hedge Liquidation	Change
Spot ($/FX)	$0.6630	$0.6829	$0.0199
Spot (FX/$)	DM1.5083	DM1.4644	–DM0.0439
Futures ($/FX)	$0.6607	$0.6823	$0.0216
# Contracts (Long)	3	3	
Spot Exposure ($)	$250,000.00	$250,000.00	$0.00
Spot Exposure (FX units)	DM377,073.91	DM366,091.17	(DM10,982.74)
Futures Values ($)	$247,762.50	$255,864.88	$8,102.38
Futures Values (FX units)			DM11,864.83
Net Results of Hedging (in FX units)			
= Futures Result + Change in Spot Exposure =			DM882.09

Effective Exchange Rate
DM1.5118/$
$0.6615/DM

Figure 12-1: Four Cases of Futures Hedging—Case III

The Short Futures Hedge—U.S. Firm

In March, a U.S. exporting firm signs a contract to sell U.S. goods and accepts DM250,000 for payment. The settlement is specified for early December.

The risk: The deutsche mark will decline in value (buying fewer dollars) between March and early December.

The solution: Sell two December DM futures contracts in March. Then, when the DM payment is received, sell the DM 250,000 to raise dollars and liquidate the futures position.

	At Hedge Initiation	At Hedge Liquidation	Change
Spot ($/FX)	$0.6107	$0.6290	$0.0183
Spot (FX/$)	DM1.6375	DM1.5898	–DM0.0477
Futures ($/FX)	$0.6045	$0.6283	$0.0238
# Contracts (Short)	2	2	
Spot Exposure (FX units)	DM250,000	DM250,000	DM0.00
Spot Exposure ($)	$152,675.00	$157,255.25	$4,580.25
Futures Values($)	$151,125.00	$157,063.67	($5,938.67)
Futures Values (FX units)			(DM11,864.83)

Net Results of Hedging
= Futures Result + Change in Spot Exposure =   ($1,358.42)

Effective Exchange Rate
$0.6053/DM
DM1.6522/$

Figure 12-1: Four Cases of Futures Hedging—Case IV

The Short Futures Hedge—Non-U.S. Firm

In early September, a Canadian importer contracts to purchase goods from a U.S. firm for a total cost of $1 million (U.S.). The settlement is specified for early December.

The risk: The value of the Canadian dollar will fall between early September and early December, converting to fewer U.S. dollars.

The solution: Sell 12 December C$ futures contracts in September. (Note: 12 contracts because $1 million ÷ ($.8237 × C$100,000) ≈ 10.) Then, when the currency is needed, sell Canadian dollars in the spot market to raise $1 million and liquidate the futures position.

	At Hedge Initiation	At Hedge Liquidation	Change
Spot ($/FX)	$0.8254	$0.8419	$0.0165
Spot (FX/$)	C$1.2115	C$1.1878	–C$0.0238
Futures ($/FX)	$0.8237	$0.8415	$0.0178
# Contracts (Short)	12	12	
Spot Exposure ($)	$1,000,000.00	$1,000,000.00	$0.00
Spot Exposure (FX units)	C$1,211,533.80	C$1,187,778.24	C$23,755.56
Futures Values ($)	$988,440.00	$1,009,783.46	($21,343.46)
Futures Values (FX units)			(C$25,351.30)
Net Results of Hedging (in FX units)			
= Futures Result + Change in Spot Exposure =			(C$1,595.74)

Effective Exchange Rate
C$1.2131/$
$0.8243/C$

Endnotes

1   It is worth noting that managers tend to look for such switching or "rolling" opportunities some weeks before the nearby futures expire.

2   The value of a tick is posted on the contract specification sheet, or it can be calculated by multiplying the size of the contract by the size of the tick. In this case, 125,000 × $0.0001 = $12.50.

3   This cost can be managed to some degree by the process of "tailing," which permits managers to offset the interest expense and income associated with variation margin. General practice tends to ignore this hedge management technique, however, as it requires substantial monitoring and adjustment. See Chapter Nineteen for a discussion on tailing, in the context of an equity exposure.

4   Again, it is important to note that the exchange rates are being discussed in American terms—dollars per other currency unit.

5   The discussion assumes that the hedge position would be held until the final settlement, when spot and futures exchange rates converge. Given a fairly stable rate differential between Eurodollar rates and the foreign counterparts, this basis will tend to converge to zero in a reasonably predictable manner. However, variability of the interest differential could add an element of uncertainty.

6   Interest rate differentials would be relevant only if the hedge were expected to be liquidated prior to the expiration of the futures contracts.

Chapter

13

Options on Currency Futures vs. Options on Physicals

A n option on a currency futures contract seems to be a somewhat esoteric financial instrument, but it is in fact more straightforward than any other alternative option vehicle in terms of pricing. For the corporate treasurer this instrument should be no more intimidating than insurance, as that is what it effectively provides.

Options come in both calls and puts, which are effective for a limited period. A June call to buy something at a fixed price, for example, would expire sometime in June. The fixed price is also referred to as the exercise or strike price. A $1.45 strike June call on a sterling futures contract would give the buyer of this option the right to purchase a June sterling futures contract at a price of $1.45/£ (for 62,500 British Pounds per contract, as each futures contract specifies a certain number of currency units). This right terminates in June.

It should be clear that the right will go unexercised if the June futures can be purchased in the open market for less than $1.45/£. This is an out-of-the-money option. If the market for June futures is trading at a price greater than $1.45, the $1.45 strike call option would be in-the-money. And finally, when the futures price equals the strike price, the option is at-the-money.

Traded on CME

As an alternative to options on futures contracts, currency managers might also consider using options on physical currency itself. The two can be used virtually interchangeably, and thus relative price considerations may be relevant for determining when to choose one over the other. Such an evaluation, however, may be complicated by the fact that two alternative options generally do not have precisely the same expirations or exercise features.

For European options (i.e., where exercise is only permitted at expiration), options on futures, and options on physical with common expiration times *should* be priced equally, since they would ultimately have the same intrinsic value at expiration. If they were not equally priced, buying the cheaper and selling the more expensive would yield a profit by the expiration date.

With both instruments, however, the price should reflect the forward premium (or discount) regardless of whether the underlying instrument is spot currency or a futures contract.

Prospect of Profits

Perhaps the point is best illustrated by an example: Suppose spot sterling were trading at $1.45/£ and the three-month forwards were $1.44/£. A three-month put option would have to cost at least $0.01/£. If it cost less, one could buy the put option and go long on the currency forward contract.

The worst possible outcome would occur if exchange rates fell by any X level below $1.44/£. The loss on the forward would be $1.44-X, but the intrinsic value of the put would be $1.45-X. The combined effect, therefore, would be to return $0.01/£ three months later. Obviously, if one paid less than $0.01/£ for this option, one would still register a profit on the trade.

In a higher exchange rate environment, on the other hand, the losses on the put would be limited, but profits on the long forward contract could soar. A declining market offers a minimal gain, and a rising market offers the prospect of large profits.

In either case, no risk is involved. Options on futures highlight this aspect of options pricing, while options on spot mask it. Without knowing the forward price, one could not tell that the put should cost at least $0.01/£, but it is obvious if the forward (futures) price is known.

While these considerations may make the option on the futures contract attractive, the real appeal of these instruments comes from what they can achieve in the way of risk management. To put it simply, owning options on futures contracts amounts to buying an insurance policy to protect against an adverse currency move.

It is common and logical to buy insurance to generate compensation if something goes wrong. A price is paid for this protection, which is an out-of-pocket expense, regardless of whether the adverse condition develops or not. Clearly, if the adverse condition does not develop, the party may be better off. For example, with fire insurance, if no fire damage occurs during the period of insurance coverage, the property may actually appreciate in value, enhancing the condition of the policy holder.

The cost of this coverage will vary, depending on the degree of damage the policy holder is willing to bear—or the deductibility of the policy. A policy with a $100 deductible clause makes the policy holder responsible for the first $100 of damage, while a $200 deductibility clause makes the policy holder responsible for $200 of damage, and so on. It should be expected that the first policy would be somewhat more expensive, since the coverage starts to pay off sooner.

The insurance paradigm serves well as a basis for understanding option purchases of both calls and puts as hedge vehicles. Like insurance, owning a call on a foreign currency futures contract pays off when the foreign currency strengthens in relation to the dollar, but the cost (analogous to the insurance premium) is limited to the price of the option. Similarly, owning a put provides a payoff when the foreign currency weakens.

The insurance paradigm generally extends to the deductibility feature, which in the options framework translates to the choice of the strike price; this last also involves a trade-off determination. An in-the-money option would be more expensive than an out-of-the-money option, reflecting the fact that protection would begin earlier.

For calls, in-the-money options would begin paying off at a lower exchange rate, (that is, in U.S. dollars per foreign currency) than out-of-the-money options, and vice versa for puts.

The choice of the strike price, therefore, effectively defines the worst-case condition for the hedge. Consider the following prices for options on deutsche mark futures:

Strike price (¢)	September calls (¢)	September puts (¢)
46	1.57/DM	0.44/DM
47	0.94	0.81
48	0.53	1.40

These call options provide a way of achieving compensation—when exchange rates rise above either $0.46, $0.47, or $0.48,—for the hedger exposed to the risk of rising deutsche marks, may be a U.S. importer or a German exporter. The true worst-case exchange rate that results, however, should reflect the cost of the "insurance" or the price of the option.

Thus, the net worst-case exchange rate that could be realized with these three options would be the strike price plus the price of the option:

46¢ strike: $0.46 + $.0157 = $0.4757
47¢ strike: $0.47 + $.0094 = $0.4794
48¢ strike: $0.48 + $.0053 = $0.4853

In the case of the hedger with the opposite need—to protect against a declining DM (for example, a U.S. exporter or a German importer)—the puts would be appropriate. The net worst-case exchange rates would be calculated by deducting the option prices from their respective strike price.

This alteration is required because the expense of the puts would reduce the number of dollars received upon the sale of the foreign currency. Given the prices shown above, the net worst-case exchange rates available are the following:

$$46¢ \text{ strike:} \quad \$0.4600 - \$0.0044 = \$0.4556$$
$$47¢ \text{ strike:} \quad \$0.4700 - \$0.0081 = \$0.4619$$
$$48¢ \text{ strike:} \quad \$0.4800 - \$0.0140 = \$0.4660$$

To illustrate the validity of these worst-case calculations, consider the hedger that chooses to buy the $0.46 strike call with the objective of locking in a worst case exchange rate of $0.4757 per deutsche mark for the purchase of DM 125,000—the precise size of one options contract.

The cost of buying one option to realize this protection would be $0.0157/DM × DM 125,000 = $1,962.50 (or 157 ticks × ($12.50/tick) = $1,962.50). Assume that the actual currency exchange is scheduled coincidentally with the option's expiration. At that time the hedger would simply purchase the desired DM 125,000 in the spot market and simultaneously realize a profit or loss on the option.

The accompanying example shown in Figure 13–1 assesses two cases—one where the spot rate has risen to $0.50/DM and one where it has fallen to $0.40/DM. For simplicity it is assumed that the futures price also moves precisely parallel to those respective rates. (The assumption can be relaxed later.)

It should be clear from Case I that no matter how high the exchange rate rises, the effective exchange rate for this hedger will always be limited to $0.4757/DM—the exchange rate designated a priori to be the worst-case condition.

Figure 13–1:
Case I: Rising Exchange Rate (Declining U.S. Dollar)

Cost of spot trade: $0.50/DM × DM 125,000	=	$62,500.00
Final call value: ($0.50/DM – $0.4600/DM) × DM 125,000	=	$5,000.00
Initial call value: $0.0157/DM × DM 125,000	=	$1,962.50
Net cost: $62,500 – $5,000 + $1,962.50	=	$59,462.50
Effective exchange rate: $\dfrac{\$59{,}462.50}{\text{DM } 125{,}000}$	=	$0.4757/DM

Note: $0.4757/DM = $0.4600/DM + $0.0157/DM

Case II: Declining Exchange Rate (Rising U.S. Dollar)

Cost of spot trade: $0.40/DM × DM 125,000	=	$50,000.00
Final call value: (no intrinsic value)	=	$0.00
Initial call value: $0.0157/DM × DM 125,000	=	$1,962.50
Net cost: $50,000 + $1,962.50	=	$51,962.50
Effective exchange rate: $\dfrac{\$51{,}962.50}{\text{DM } 125{,}000}$	=	$0.4157

If exchange rates decline, however, as shown in Case II, this hedger will achieve the more beneficial exchange rate net of the cost of the protection.

Two wild cards in the pack might cause some difference in the outcome from the results that would otherwise be anticipated by the above procedure. First, given that the option on currency futures do not expire coincidentally with their underlying futures, the assumption of perfect convergence between spot and futures prices is unrealistic.

Although the difference would probably be small, the earlier results can be modified by a straightforward adjustment to take account of this condition. The effective exchange rate result will be the appropriate calculation as already shown, in other words, depending on whether using a put or a call, minus any basis expected at expiration that is not reflected in the intrinsic value of the option.

Second, if the proposed currency exchange is scheduled for a date prior to the options' expiration, the option will have time left to expiration. The option results will be unambiguously improved by the amount of the time value at liquidation.

Pleasant Surprise

Of the two uncertainties mentioned—the basis condition and the remaining time value—the second, which is always beneficial, could easily have far greater consequences. Even so, the amount of the time value that will be available is completely uncertain. It may be considerable if liquidation occurs when the option is at-the-money, but with deep in-the-money and deep out-of-the-money options, it could be negligible.

As a rule, hedgers want to understand their worst-case possibilities. The seemingly naive calculations already outlined, with a simple adjustment for a worst-case liquidation basis, offer the desired information since they assume no additional time value in the option's returns.

More likely than not, however, with this worst-case benchmark in mind, the long option hedger is likely to be pleasantly surprised by actual hedge outcomes in most cases—whether the "insurance" pays off, or not.

This chapter is based on *Corporate Finance*, "An Insurance Policy that Covers Forex Exposure," October 1986, a Euromoney Publication.

Chapter

14

Applications for Options on Currency Futures

Most professional foreign exchange managers initially investigate options contracts because of the need to manage an existing foreign exchange rate exposure. In this case, the use of options is quite conservative because they are employed to offset the pre-existing risk facing the financial manager. At the other extreme, however, options may also be used to take on risk for the express purpose of generating profits. In this latter case, options function as a trading vehicle, and the liquidity of the exchange-traded options markets provides the kind of flexibility and easy access that is quite attractive to those with this orientation.

This chapter provides a concise, largely conceptual overview of these two different orientations to the marketplace. First, it describes the most fundamental way in which hedgers use options; second, it explains how volatility is connected to options pricing; and finally, it discusses the issue of options trading, which, as one might guess, is intimately tied to issues pertaining to volatility.

Options Hedging Strategies

Options limit potential risks to which one is exposed, but they do so for a cost. The purchase of a call option on a currency futures contract provides an offset for the effect of a strengthening non-U.S. currency (i.e., a weakening dollar). Although this strategy allows the manager to limit risk, the market must move beyond a certain threshold if the option is held to its expiration in order for the option to pay off. Alternatively, a put option on a currency futures provides an offset for a weakening non-U.S. currency (i.e., a strengthening dollar). Conceptually, there is the analogous arrangement: One can limit one's risk with this vehicle, and a payoff is generated when the market goes down below some threshold.

Consider the situation of an unhedged foreign exchange rate manager who is exposed to the risk of a weakening dollar. In Figure 14–1, the price of foreign exchange in American terms is shown on the horizontal axis. Moving to the right shows strengthening foreign exchange or a weakening dollar. Moving to the left shows the reverse. If the foreign exchange manager bears this exposure, whether because of the transaction or because of translations consideration, the exchange rate move is either going to make money or cost money. Essentially, this position is nothing more than a speculation that the dollar will strengthen. So what can one do?

One could cover that exposure using futures contracts. By hedging with futures, one neutralizes both the risk and the opportunity. An alternative for covering this type of exposure is to use a long call instead of using a long futures contract. If the dollar were to weaken, the option would pay back for the loss that one would make on one's normal exposure. On the other hand, if the market were to move the other way, one would be out the cost of the option, but one might still benefit from the

Figure 14–1: Exposure to the Risk of a Weakening Dollar

This unhedged FX manager is exposed to the risk of a weakening dollar and the opportunity of a strengthening dollar.

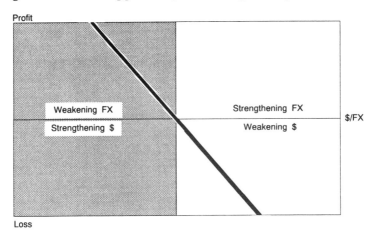

exchange rate move. In other words, by covering with a long call, one can limit the risk and still maintain opportunity. Thus, the effect of buying a call on a currency futures contract is to create a ceiling rate on a forthcoming exchange transaction, with the ceiling rate determined by the exercise price of the option (the exchange rate at which the underlying futures can be purchased) adjusted for the cost of the option itself.[1] When dealing with the opposite exposure, one could manage the exchange rate risk by using the short futures contract or else a long put to get similar choices. In this case, the purchase of a put results in the creation of a floor on the forthcoming exchange rate, or a minimum exchange rate, expressed in American terms.

Issues of Volatility

Although most managers who deal with options recognize that option prices can be divided between time and intrinsic value, many ignore the fact that time value reflects more than just the length of time remaining until expiration. That is, it also reflects volatility considerations. It should be clear that the greater the volatility of any market, the greater are the chances that an option trader can liquidate a trade at a profit. For that reason, greater volatility translates into a higher option price, all else being equal. In the short run, this determinant may exert such an important effect on option prices that it can outweigh the effect of a market move.

Volatility is measured and expressed as an annualized percentage. A measure of volatility of, say, 10 percent implies a 67 percent probability that the price will change by no more than 10 percent within a year's time, a 95 percent probability that the price change will be within 20 percent (2 × 10 percent), and a 99.7 percent probability that the change will be within 30 percent (3 × 10 percent).

To be precise, one should distinguish between historical volatility and implied volatility. Past data are used to calculate a measure of historical volatility, or how variable the price history of the underlying market has been over some earlier period (for example, the past 20 days, 60 days, or whatever). Typically, this measure is simply the standard deviation of the daily returns exhibited by the price series multiplied by the square root of 250, which effectively annualizes the figure.[2] Implied volatility is the variable that is derived from the observed option price. That is, given a formula for the determination of the option price (such as the Black-Scholes formula), one could work backward, plugging in all remaining variables to solve for the volatility that would be required to generate an option model prediction equal to the current market price of the option.

Importantly, nothing directly ties implied volatility to historical volatility. In other words, at any time, these two values could be significantly different from each other. Moreover, it is conceivable that historical volatility might be on a declining path while implied volatility is rising. No mechanism in the marketplace necessarily forces the two to come together. Thus, although many market participants have a natural interest in historical volatility, the implied volatility is in fact the market determinant that has the greatest impact on an options price. For that reason, a projection of implied volatility carries great importance for the option trader.

Failure to consider implied volatility could have dire consequences for the short-term option trader. For example, suppose a trader bought a call in the expectation of a rising market. Conceivably, the market could rise, but simultaneously volatility could fall in such a way that the rise in intrinsic value would be offset by the greater decline in time value. In such a case, the trader would be right on the direction of the market but wrong on volatility, and a loss would result.

Trading Technique

Given the importance of volatility, it is reasonable to consider trading based on expected changes in implied volatility, independent of changes in market levels of the underlying futures. That is, if one expects a rise in volatility, one would buy options (either puts or calls). Conversely, if one thinks volatility is likely to fall, one would sell options. In either case, if one is a pure volatility trader, one would take the second step of insulating the position from the effects of price level adjustments of the underlying futures contract.

The principal way traders take advantage of an expected change in volatility involves a process called *delta hedging*. The

delta is the movement expected in the price of the option relative to the price of the underlying instrument. Delta absolute
values fall within a range of zero to one. For example, prices of
at-the-money options[3] generally change about half as much as
the price of their underlying currencies (or futures), making the
delta about 50 percent for an at-the-money option. In-the-money
options have higher deltas, and out-of-the-money options have
lower deltas. The deeper in-the-money the option is, the closer
the delta is to unity (or 100 percent) in absolute value, whereas
the more out-of-the-money an option is, the closer the delta is to
zero. At any time, the appropriate size of the spot position
should equal the delta multiplied by the face value of the option
exposure. Thus, whether one is a buyer of options or a seller of
options, one can offset the market impact of a change in the
underlying futures price by delta hedging.

Consider what can happen if one predicts a decline in implied volatility and the following market conditions exist for
deutsche mark futures and options:

	Prices
46-call	1.68¢
47-call	1.01
48-call	0.55
Futures	$0.4736

If one chooses to sell the 47-call as a volatility trade, one
needs to buy futures in a proportion dictated by the delta of the
47-call option, which would be generated with the aid of an
option pricing model.

As the underlying exchange rate rises (again in American
terms), however, the call option will be moving deeper in-the-
money, and thus the delta of the call option will be rising as
well. (Puts will be moving out-of-the-money, and their deltas
will be declining.) As a consequence, the price change in the
value of the futures position will not match the change in the

value of the options position. To hedge appropriately, therefore, one needs to adjust the hedge position as the underlying exchange rate varies.

Table 14–1 shows the deltas for a $1.2250 strike call option with one month until expiration and with one week until expiration, over a range of prices for the spot exchange rate. In addition to demonstrating the rather significant sensitivity of the delta to changing market conditions, the table also shows a similar sensitivity to time. That is, even if the market does not change, the mere passage of time will foster the need for readjusting. For in-the-money options, deltas will rise with the passage of time, requiring ever-increasing hedge positions (all else remaining equal), whereas for out-of-the-money options, deltas will fall, requiring a reduction of hedge positions.

The difficulty in such trading practices is knowing when to adjust. Whether the market goes up or down, failure to adjust

Table 14–1: Theoretical Deltas

Spot Price	Percentage Change in Spot Price	CME Options Deltas ($1.2250–Strike)	
		One Month Before Expiration	One Week Before Expiration
1.1070	−10.00	15.48%	0.51%
1.1378	−7.50	23.21	3.09
1.1685	−5.00	32.44	11.75
1.1993	−2.50	42.61	29.97
1.2300	0.00	53.00	54.77
1.2607	2.50	62.91	77.28
1.2915	5.00	71.79	91.28
1.3223	7.50	79.28	97.40
1.3530	10.00	85.26	99.33

the hedge may result in losses—unless the market reverses itself. [4] Moreover, even if a reversal occurs, if such a reversal follows an adjustment, the hedger suffers from whipsaw losses. For example, suppose the market rallies, calling for additional long futures. Then suppose the market drops back. Upon rebalancing the delta hedge a second time, one realizes losses on the "extra" futures sold at a lower price. Thus, although volatility trading may offer some attractive profit opportunities, that outcome is by no means certain. The growth of these markets, however, suggests that the opportunities have been ample, and perhaps worth a look.

This chapter is reprinted from *International Capital Markets: New Directions* (1989) with permission from the New York Institute of Finance.

Endnotes

1 The ceiling rate is a maximum exchange rate when expressed in American terms (i.e., dollars per non-U.S. currency unit).

2 Various models may have a somewhat different multiplier to the standard deviation, depending on the number of observations per year. For example, a model using weekly data would have a multiplier of the square root of 52.

3 An "at-the-money option" is an option that has a strike price equal to the current market value of the underlying instrument (e.g., $1.2500 strike option on the British pound futures is at-the-money when pound futures are trading at $1.2500 per unit). When pound futures are trading higher, the $1.2500 strike call is in-the-money and the put is out-of-the-money. When pound futures are less, the $1.2500 strike call

is out-of-the-money, and the $1.2500 strike put is in-the-money.

4   Consider the case of hedging short calls with futures, with a rising market and no hedge ratio adjustment. As the delta of the calls increases, losses on the calls will exceed gains on futures. In a declining market, as the delta of the calls decreases, gains on the calls will fall short of the losses on the futures. In contrast, delta hedging long option positions permits profits to accrue when markets move either way but no hedge ratio adjustment is made. This latter opportunity comes at a cost, however, maintaining long options will "cost" the holder the eroding time and value.

Chapter

15

Trading Cross-Rates with Inter-Currency Spreads

I nter-market spreads created with dollar-based currency futures contracts offer an opportunity to profit from cross-
currency exchange rate moves. This chapter explores these
spreads and explains how to structure such a trade. It also
highlights some aspects of the trade that must be understood to
achieve the desired results.

Explanation of Cross-Currency Futures Spread

The cross-currency futures spread requires buying (going long)
in one currency and selling (going short) in another. Suppose,
for example, that currency A is expected to strengthen in relation to currency B.[1] In that case, one would buy currency A
futures and sell currency B futures. Profits would accrue under
three alternative scenarios as follows:

1. Both currently A and currency B strengthen with respect to the dollar, with currency A strengthening
   more.
2. Both currency A and currency B weaken with respect to
   the dollar, with currency A weakening less.

3. Currency A strengthens in relation to the dollar, and currency B weakens in relation to the dollar.

In the first two instances, one leg of the spread would win and the other would lose, with profits outpacing losses for a net gain. In the third case, both legs of the spread would generate gains. The reverse trade (long currency B/short currency A) would produce profits under the three opposite rate movement scenarios. Intended results would be guaranteed only if the contracts are traded in the correct proportion. Put another way, one could correctly anticipate the cross-rate move but generate losses on a trade of incorrect proportions.

Designing the Trade

Correctly designing the position requires that an equal dollar value be used on each side of the spread. The respective dollar values should be calculated by multiplying the contract size by the appropriate futures price. Assume prices of $0.5625 for German marks and $0.008277 for Japanese yen, for example. Given the contract sizes of 125,000 marks per mark contract and 12.5 million yen per yen contract, the dollar values are $70,312.50 (125,000 × 0.5625) and $103,462.50 (12,500,000 × 0.008277), respectively. Let A* be the number of mark contracts required and B* be the number of yen contracts required. The ratio of A* to B* can be determined by the following equation:

$$A^* \times \$70{,}312.50 = B^* \times \$103{,}462.50$$

In this case A*/B* equals approximately 1.5. Thus, the appropriate trade proportion would be 1.5 to 1 (or 3 to 2) contracts of mark to yen futures.

Significant Considerations

It is important to remember that the desired hedge ratio is a moving target. As one or both currency values change in relation to the dollar, the associated dollar values will change in direct proportion. This concern would not affect a pre-existing trade, but it would dictate a change in trade proportions for subsequent trades following price adjustments. Another important consideration deals with the existence of a basis in this trade. This point can be illustrated using the following example. Spot and futures prices for currencies A and B, in American terms, are as follows:

	Mark	Yen
Spot prices	0.5595	0.008258
Futures prices	0.5625	0.008277

Using spot market prices, the mark/yen ratio or cross-rate is 67.75; using futures prices, it is 67.96. Given that the futures market must converge to the spot, the starting basis favors the short mark/long yen position. This occurs because short mark/long yen would make money if there were no changes in the spot market prices. If futures were to converge to the existing spot prices, the short mark/long yen position traded in a 3-to-2 ratio would generate a profit of $650. This is demonstrated in scenario C of Table 15–1. Although this "basis bias" needs to be recognized, it may not be overriding. If one expected a mark/yen ratio to rise above 67.96 by the contracts' expiration date, the appropriate trade would be long mark/short yen in spite of the disadvantageous basis. Thus, the starting basis may be considered a hurdle (when adverse) or an added benefit (when attractive). Therefore, it makes sense to understand which situation exists at the time one puts on the trade.

Table 15–1: Cross-Currency Spread Example

Outlook: Bearish on DM relative to JY

Actions: Sell 3 DM futures @ $0.5625
                Buy 2 JY futures @ $0.008277

Starting cross-rate = 0.5625/0.008277 = 67.96

$$\boxed{\text{Profit} = +/- \text{ contracts} \times \text{price change} \times \text{ contract size}}$$

Possible Outcomes

Scenario A: DM settles @ $0.6188
                JY settles @ $0.009520
                DM/JY = 65.00

DM Futures: −3 × (0.6188 − 0.5625) × 125,000=   −$21,112.50
JY Futures: +2 × (0.009520 − 0.008277) × 12,500,000 =   31,075.00
                                                    Combined: $ 9,962.50

Scenario B: DM settles @ $0.5063
                JY settles @ $0.007789
                DM/JY = 65.00

DM Futures: −3 × (0.5063 − 0.5625) × 125,000 = $21,075.00
JY Futures: +2 × (0.007789 − 0.008277) × 12,500,000 =   −$12,200.00
                                                    Combined: $ 8,875.00

Table continues

Scenario C: DM settles @ $0.5595

JY settles @ $0.008258

DM/JY = 67.75

DM Futures: −3 × (0.5595 − 0.5625) × 125,000 = $ 1,125.00

JY Futures: +2 × (0.008258 − 0.008277) × 12,500,000 =   =$ 475.00

Combined: $ 650.00

_____

The results shown in scenario A and B reflect a weakening of DM versus JY under two alternative price paths: a 10 percent rise in the DM futures price (scenario A) and a 10 percent decline in DM futures price (scenario B), with appropriate adjustments in the JY futures price to reduce the final DM/JY ratio to 65.00 in both cases. Note that the respective profits vary depending on the way in which this adjustment occurs. Scenario C shows the profit associated with the convergence of the futures prices to the spot prices that were available at the initiation of the trace.

Conclusion

The use of cross-currency spreads to profit from anticipated changes offers attractive profit opportunities, but the trade design requires significant thought and attention. An outcome consistent with expectations can be assured only by balancing the trade properly. Evaluation of the cross-rates indicated by spot prices compared with cross-rates indicated by futures prices may offer clues as to when such futures spreads may be particularly attractive or unattractive. Understanding both of these issues will undoubtedly result in uncovering enticing trade possibilities that may be of use to the asset/liability manager.

This chapter is reprinted from *Bank Asset/Liability Management* (May 1989) © 1989 Warren, Gorham & Lamont Inc. Used with permission.

Endnote

1 Both A and B futures are assumed to be dollar-based (i.e., neither is a cross-rate futures contract).

Chapter

16

Managing Currency Risks
of
Non-Dollar Portfolios

W   *ith the availability of currency hedging instruments—*
including futures, forwards, and options contracts—
foreign exchange risk can be isolated from the price
risk of the investment evaluated in its home (non-dol-
lar) currency. Managers can thus choose to regulate their currency
exposure as conditions dictate. At one extreme, they may choose to
maintain their exchange exposure intact; at the other, they may elimi-
nate it entirely.

U.S. investors dealing in non-dollar securities face two risks—the market risk of the investment in its home currency and dollar/non-dollar exchange rate risk. When the non-dollar currency is strengthening in relation to the dollar, this latter consideration may add to the desirability of the non-dollar investment. But suppose the non-dollar currency starts to weaken. What does the investor do then? Of course, he or she can sell the investment(s) and repatriate the currency back to dollars, but depending on the bid/ask spreads on the individual instruments and the currency itself, as well as the commissions involved, such an adjustment might be expensive—especially if the shift back into dollars ends up being reversed in the near future.

The alternative to liquidating the portfolio is to hedge the currency exposure by (1) selling currency futures, (2) buying puts on currency futures, or (3) selling calls. The choice depends on one's expectations about the size of the anticipated exchange rate change as well as one's appetite for risk. In all cases, however, the quantity of non-dollar currency units exposed to risk will be a moving target, rising or falling as the non-dollar value of the portfolio increases or decreases, respectively. The appropriate *hedge ratio* should thus be recalculated on an ongoing basis, and adjustments should be made as needed.

Consider a portfolio of German securities, originally valued at DM5 million. If the manager decides to hedge the currency exposure with futures, the appropriate hedge would be found simply by taking the value of the portfolio in marks and dividing by the size of the mark futures contract (DM125,000). The initial hedge would thus require selling 40 deutsche mark futures.

Table 16–1 shows the outcome of the hedged portfolio over three periods (i.e., from T0 through T3). During each period, the mark-denominated value of the portfolio increases by 2.5 percent. At the same time, the dollar value of a mark drops by $0.02.[1] If no currency hedge had been put in place, the net result of the market change would have been a decline in the dollar value of the portfolio of slightly less than 1 percent over the entire period. With a hedge that is adjusted upward each period as the mark-denominated value of the portfolio moves higher, the dollar value of the portfolio rises from $3.75 million to $4.0 million—a gain of about 7.3 percent.

Had the currency remained stable, the value of the portfolio would have risen by almost 7.7 percent. The hedge thus allowed the investor to enjoy almost all the non-currency-based market appreciation. The small shortfall is a result of the fact that the hedge ratio is always adjusted somewhat belatedly; and prior to each adjustment, the investor is slightly under-hedged. Under such conditions, the compensation generated by the hedge falls slightly short of the damage done by the weakening mark.

Table 16-1: Hedging the Currency Exposure of a Non-Dollar Portfolio When Foreign Exchange Is Weakening

	T0	T1	T2	T3
Portfolio Value (DM)	5,000,000	5,125,000	5,253,125	5,384,453
Portfolio Growth Rate (DM)				
Per Period	—	2.50%	2.50%	2.50%
Cumulative	—	2.50%	5.06%	7.69%
Spot Exchange ($/DM)	0.7500	0.7300	0.7100	0.6900
Portfolio Value ($)	3,750,000	3,741,250	3,729,719	3,715,273
Portfolio Growth Rate ($)				
Per Period	—	−0.23%	−0.31%	−0.39%
Cumulative	—	−0.23%	−0.54%	−0.93%
DM Futures Price	0.7500	0.7300	0.7100	0.6900
DM Contract Size	125,000	125,000	125,000	125,000
Theoretical Hedge Ratio (No. Short Contracts)	40.0	41.0	42.0	43.1
Actual Hedge Ratio	40	41	42	43
Results (Individual Periods)				
DM Futures	—	100,000	102,500	105,000
Portfolio Change ($)	—	−8,750	−11,531	−14,446
Combined	—	91,250	90,969	90,554
Hedged Portfolio Growth Rate	—	2.43%	2.43%	2.43%
Results (Cumulative)				
DM Futures	—	100,000	202,500	307,500
Portfolio Change ($)	—	−8,750	−20,281	−34,727
Combined	—	91,250	182,219	252,773
Hedged Portfolio ($)	—	3,841,250	3,932,219	4,022,773
Hedged Portfolio Growth Rate	—	2.43%	4.86%	7.27%

Table 16–2 shows the potential outcome if the currency becomes stronger—contrary to the hedger's expectations. In this
case, the hedge immunizes the investor from the beneficial effect
of the rising value of the mark. The final result shows a cumulative growth rate of 8.1 percent for the hedged portfolio, which is
slightly better than the 7.7 percent growth of the mark-denominated portfolio independent of currency considerations. Again,
the difference arises because of the imperfect hedge adjustment
process; this time, however, the underhedging is beneficial, as
the futures contracts are generating losses.

Choppy markets create a problem for the dynamic hedge
adjustment process. Consider, for example, a non-dollar portfolio whose value rises and falls multiple times because of volatility in its home market. The dollar-based investor would
probably increase and decrease the size of his or her hedge ac-
cordingly. The profits or losses on such adjustments would depend on the level of the exchange rate at the time of each trade;
and, of course, one couldn't know in advance how serious (or
beneficial) this aspect of the hedge would be. In all cases, however, the effect of commissions and bid/ask spreads would be
detrimental. Thus, if sufficient volatility develops, whipsaw
losses on the hedge could be a problem.

The discussion above pertains to a dynamic hedge using
futures, but parallel cases can be shown for long put hedges or
short call hedges. In both of these cases, the proper size of the
hedge rises and falls as the non-dollar currency exposure increases and decreases. Ideally, a dynamic long put hedge will
protect the portfolio from the potential adverse effects of a
weakening non-dollar currency (strengthening dollar) and will
allow the benefits of a strengthening currency (weakening dollar). A short call hedge will generate immediate revenue from
the sale of the option, providing a finite dollar value of protection. At the same time, it will commit the hedger to forgoing the
benefit of a strengthening non-dollar currency. As is the case
with the dynamic futures hedge, these two alternative hedging

Table 16–2: Hedging the Currency Exposure of a Non-Dollar Portfolio When Foreign Exchange Is Strengthening

	T0	T1	T2	T3
Portfolio Value (DM)	5,000,000	5,125,000	5,253,125	5,384,453
Portfolio Growth Rate (DM)				
Per Period		2.50%	2.50%	2.50%
Cumulative		2.50%	5.06%	7.69%
Spot Exchange ($/DM)	0.7500	0.7700	0.7900	0.8100
Portfolio Value ($)	3,750,000	3,946,250	4,149,969	4,361,407
Portfolio Growth Rate ($)				
Per Period		5.23%	5.16%	5.09%
Cumulative		5.23%	10.67%	16.30%
DM Futures Price	0.7500	0.7700	0.7900	0.8100
DM Contract Size	125,000	125,000	125,000	125,000
Theoretical Hedge Ratio				
(No. Short Contracts)	40.0	41.0	42.0	43.1
Actual Hedge Ratio	40	41	42	43
Results (Individual Periods)				
DM Futures	—	−100,000	−102,500	−105,000
Portfolio Change ($)	—	196,250	203,719	211,438
Combined	—	96,250	101,219	106,438
Hedged Portfolio Growth Rate	—	2.57%	2.56%	2.56%
Results (Cumulative)				
DM Futures	—	−100,000	−202,500	−307,500
Portfolio Change ($)	—	196,250	399,969	611,407
Combined	—	96,250	197,469	303,907
Hedged Portfolio ($)	—	3,846,250	3,947,469	4,053,907
Hedged Portfolio Growth Rate	—	2.57%	5.27%	8.10%

strategies have a certain amount of inherent uncertainty because of the imperfect adjustment procedure and the potential for whipsaw losses.

Conclusion

While available exchange-traded currency hedging instruments may not achieve perfect currency exchange rate protection, they do offer the manager of non-dollar investments some valuable flexibility. The manager who rules out such hedging devices is left with the choice of either liquidating investments or sweating out periods of declines in non-dollar currencies. Dynamic foreign exchange hedging expands investment alternatives and thus offers opportunities for enhanced performance.

Conceptually (or ideally), selling futures locks in the currency exchange rate, thereby eliminating both risk and opportunity. Buying puts protects against adverse currency exchange rate moves but leaves open the possibility of a beneficial change—for a price. Selling calls generates income, hence offering a finite amount of protection from an adverse move, but also obligating the hedger to forgo improved performance associated with a beneficial foreign exchange move.

In all cases, the hedger can expect to approach the ideal, but practical considerations will necessarily create some uncertainty. Deviations from the ideal could prove to be either beneficial or adverse. In general, however, the potential discrepancy will appear to be a relatively minor consideration when compared with either the cost of liquidating a portfolio or the risk of holding it unhedged.

This chapter is reprinted from *Financial Analysts Journal* (May-June 1991). Permission granted by Financial Analysts Federation, 1991.

Endnote

1 For simplicity, the example equates spot and futures prices and thus ignores basis risk.

Part

III

Stock Indexes

Chapter

17

Speculating

T he most straightforward application for stock index futures is speculation. Ultimately, this use boils down to placing the proper bet on the direction of the market. In other words, it's the old "buy low, sell high" approach. In spite of the simplicity of the strategy, a high degree of sophistication may be employed. It is the purpose of this chapter to identify a number of valuation practices—both quantitative and subjective—to help in the speculative trading strategy.

First, we will examine the trading history of the Standard & Poor's 500 Composite Index, the New York Stock Exchange Composite Index, and the Value Line Average Composite. That history and other structural conditions have a bearing on the choice of a contract for speculative purposes. Second, we will identify and evaluate several basic speculative strategies. The chapter concludes with a summary and some cautionary remarks concerning speculative activities.

Factors Bearing on the Choice of a Contract for Speculative Purposes

Trading History

Despite the conceptual and practical differences among the underlying stock indices, a historical view of the price performance of these indices shows no *consistent* bias in the way the three comprehensive indices—NYSE, S&P 500, and Value Line—perform. Virtually no general rule can be made as to which of the underlying indices will exhibit the greatest move at a particular time—in either bull or bear markets. This conclusion is supported by Figures 17–1 and 17–2.

For Figure 17–1, quarter-end data are used for the period 1971 through 1982. Each of the three indices is re-indexed, with March 31, 1971, set equal to 1.00. Shown on the chart are the

Figure 17–1:
Stock Market Indexes, Natural Logarithm
End-of-Quarter Close*

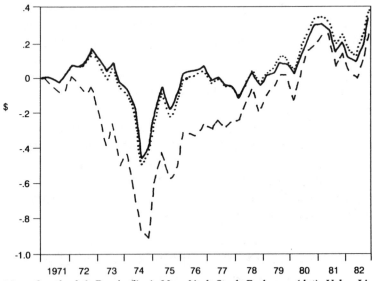

Note: Standard & Poor's (line), New York Stock Exchange (dot), Value Line (dash).

*Reindexed: March 31, 1971 = 1.00.

plots of the natural logs of the re-based indices. When the plotting is done in natural logarithm form, the slopes of the lines reflect the respective rates of growth of the three underlying indices. The steeper the slope, the faster the rate of change of the underlying index, and vice versa.

Two conclusions stand out. First, the S&P index and the NYSE index performed in very similar fashions, while the Value Line index showed numerous periods of contrary movement. Second, and more subtle, the behavior of the Value Line index relative to that of the other two indices is inconsistent. Look, for example, at the periods in which both the S&P index and the NYSE index declined (1973-74, 1977, and 1980-82). In the first decline, the Value Line index dropped most steeply; in the second, the Value Line index actually rose; and in the third, all three indices experienced comparable declines.

Shifting the focus to the short run, Figure 17–2 shows daily percentage changes for each of the three comprehensive (unadjusted) indices. On a daily basis, hardly any difference in the performance of the indices is noticeable for the period July-December 1982. They all behaved similarly.

The point is that with any single speculative effort, none of the underlying indices can be counted upon with certainty to have the largest percentage change in its value. Sometimes the largest change will occur for one index, sometimes for another. Put differently, from the price history it appears that any of the three indices can be used for speculative purposes, and one cannot tell before the event which of the indices will move the most for any given market change.

If price performance does not seem to be a helpful differentiating factor for deciding which contract should be traded, how should the decision be made? Two factors are suggested below relating to liquidity and margin requirements and their impact on leverage.

Figure 17–2:
Stock Market Indexes, Percent Change, Daily Close

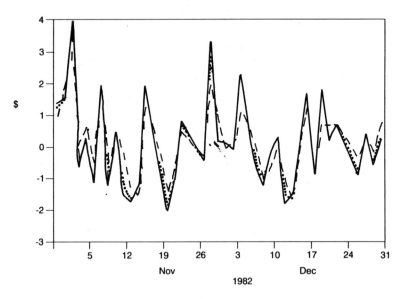

Note: Standard & Poor's (line), New York Stock Exchange (dot), Value Line (dash).

Liquidity

To compare liquidity for the three contracts, two different indicators are used: volume and open interest. Volume measures the number of contracts that are traded in the course of a day, while open interest gives a reading on the depth of the market by counting the number of contracts outstanding at the end of the day. Figure 17–3 plots the average daily volume of the three contracts from the onset of trading through the end of 1982.

Clearly, the Standard & Poor's contract has the highest trading volume. The New York Stock Exchange contract has

Figure 17-3: Stock Market Indexes, Average Volume

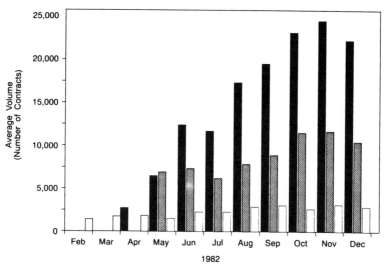

Note: Standard & Poor's (black), New York Stock Exchange (shaded), Value Line (clear).

grown in volume, too, albeit at a more modest pace; but volume at the Kansas City Board of Trade, where the Value Line contract trades, appears to have leveled out. In Figure 17-4 open interest is shown. By this measure of liquidity, the Standard & Poor's contract is again the most liquid of the three, the NYSE contract is next, and the Value Line contract is third.

These two measures of liquidity are relevant because they give an indication of a capacity to enter and exit from a futures position without disrupting the market. As a general rule, as volume and open interest rise, there is a decline in the potential of any single market order to affect the price of futures. For this reason, all else being equal, market participants prefer to trade in markets with higher volume and open interest. They also

Figure 17–4: Stock Market Indexes, Average Open Interest

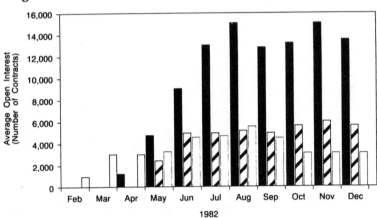

Note: Standard & Poor's (black), New York Stock Exchange (striped), Value Line (clear).

tend to shy away from relatively less active markets because liquidity is dynamic. That is, although sufficient volume and open interest exist at the time the futures position is initiated, during any period in which that position is open, one faces the risk that liquidity will diminish by the time termination of the position is desired.

Given market participants' preference for trading in the market with the highest volume, order flow naturally tends to gravitate to that market, reinforcing the liquidity of ordering. Therefore, as the most liquid contract, the S&P future has a clear advantage over the two other stock index futures.

Margin and Leverage

A second differentiating factor among the index futures contracts relates to margin requirements—the initial margin requirement and the ratio between the value of the margin and the value of the underlying contracts. The initial margin requirement is important because it reflects the capital needed to initiate a futures position.

Aside from the issue of the amount of capital needed in order to speculate, initial margin is important because it has a bearing on leverage. The lower the ratio of the initial margin requirement to the value of the underlying contract, the greater the leverage offered by the contract. The reciprocal of this ratio indicates the amount of contract value that can be purchased for a given dollar of initial margin. For example, suppose that the Value Line, S&P, and NYSE indices were trading at 167.40, 145.72, and 84.16, respectively. Since each contract is equal to 500 times the underlying index, the contract values would be $83,700, $72,860, and $42,080.[1] These respective values divided by their associated initial margin requirements yield a measure of contract value for each dollar of initial margin. As the market moves or as initial margin requirements change, the degree of leverage associated with the three contracts will vary.

More leverage, of course, means greater rewards for a given movement in the futures price; however, it also means more risk. Therefore, it is not clear whether the higher leverage should be favored by speculators. The preference will be highly individual.

The foregoing discussion focused on structural considerations that speculators should confront: how the respective underlying stock indices move, liquidity, and margin requirements and their impact on leverage. Now we turn to more quantitative and strategic concerns.

Speculative Strategies

First, let us review the opening position in the futures market that should be taken based on the speculator's expectations about the movement of "the market." If the speculator expects a rise in the market, the speculator should buy the futures contract (that is, take a long position). On the other hand, if the speculator expects a decline in the market, the speculator should sell the futures contract (that is, take a short position). The speculator will realize a gain if the market moves in the direction anticipated, but he or she will pay the piper if the market moves in the opposite direction.

In discussing speculative trading strategies, it is helpful to focus on the duration of the holding period. One who intends to speculate on broad market moves that are expected over weeks and months will base his or her trading decisions on technical and fundamental considerations (i.e., analysis of existing conditions and trends in the stock market and in the economy as a whole). It is not the intention of this chapter to explain this type of research and the long-term position taken. Rather, we focus on those who trade with a more rapid round-trip period—for example, on an intra-day or overnight basis. Such traders will employ additional considerations in their trading decisions. In this chapter two specific strategies are suggested for the short-term speculator. Both these strategies involve tracking the underlying stock index for any of the three stock futures; therefore, to speculate with these strategies, one must have access to a quote vending machine—either directly or through a broker.

The first strategy simply relies on a traditional commodity trading maxim—"Go with the trend." Although the market may have a number of peaks and troughs during any given day, by and large it is fairly easy to categorize the short-run action as rising, flat, or declining. A tick-by-tick chart (see Figure 17–5) shows the relative smoothness of an underlying index, in this case the S&P, compared to the futures. The idea, then, is simply *to determine the direction of the trend in the stock market. Go long the futures on market rises and short the futures on market declines. The position should be maintained only as long as the actual market continues its trend.* At any market leveling or trend reversal, the

Figure 17–5:
Example of Intra-day Prices, S&P 500 Composite Index and December 82 Futures Contract, Final Trading Day, December 16, 1982

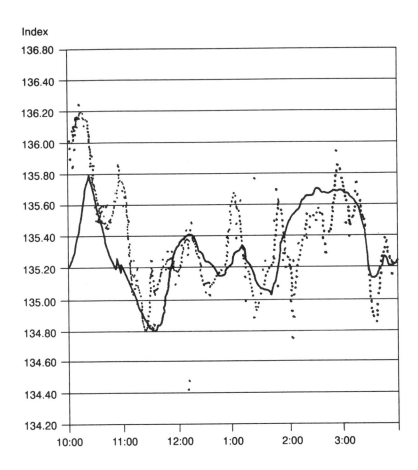

Source: ADP Comtrend.

futures position should be liquidated. As Figure 17–5 demonstrates, this strategy is not without its pitfalls. Specifically, profits cannot be realized unless the market undergoes a sustained move, and short-run ups and downs may result in a rapid turnover of futures positions that could generate cumulative losses. Moreover, even when the market does move decidedly in one direction, sometimes the futures move perversely. A good case in point occurred around 2 P.M. on the day shown on Figure 17–5.

The second strategy involves a more selective process of timing futures positions and mitigates some of the above shortcomings. First, let us consider a bull market scenario, where the basis is at a premium. Even in bull markets, there tend to be short-run periods where the actual stock market goes into a decline. When this happens, the basis usually shrinks. *The strategy, therefore, is to wait for basis conditions in which the basis appears to be atypically high (judgmentally) and then to enter a short futures position as soon as the market moves downward. The short position should be maintained only as long as the downward direction of the actual stock market is observed.* If the uptrend resumes or if the market stays flat, the short position should be dropped.

This strategy works in reverse during a bear market. The speculator waits until the basis is atypically wide—at a discount this time—and exercises a long position during an upward correction. Again, the position is liquidated when the underlying stock market resumes its bearish direction. Returning again to Figure 17–5, at least two and possibly three opportunities to implement this strategy arose on the day shown—at about 11, after 2, and perhaps near the close, at about 3:40. In each case the suggested strategy would have been successful.

Characteristically, the transition from bear market to bull market, or vice versa, comes with little advance notice. Thus, this strategy would conceivably put someone in position to capture a downward move from the peak or an upward move from the trough, earning the original atypically wide basis in addition to the magnitude of the market move. Moreover, it is conceivable that aside from earning the initial basis, a second advantageous basis could be captured as the change in expectations moves the basis from premium to discount in going from a bull market to a bear market (or from discount to premium going from a bear market to a bull market).

In both of these strategies one must literally follow the index recalculations as they occur. Moreover, the speculator must recognize that he or she is essentially playing probabilities. Clearly, there will be times when markets are choppy and when, because the market never undergoes any significant change, futures positions will be executed with little or no profit. The speculator must be prepared, therefore, to withstand a certain amount of loss in order to be positioned for major moves when they do develop. Either of the two strategies, as described above, if adhered to with discipline, will tend to limit losses and allow profits to accumulate. In the long run, both strategies should lead to desirable results.

Conclusion

This chapter considers short-run speculative trading strategies, focusing on three fundamental decisions (1) which of the available index futures contracts should be chosen as the vehicle for speculation, (2) upon which direction of the market one should speculate, and (3) when one should enter (and exit from) the market.

With respect to the issue of which contract to choose, the speculator must evaluate trade-offs between liquidity and margin requirements (and their impact on leverage opportunities). Two specific strategies are explained that emphasize the trends of the underlying indices and the opportunities created by a variable basis—the difference between the future and its underlying stock index.

Despite the reasonableness of the strategies outlined, no chapter on speculation would be complete without ample words of caution. Stock index futures offer some very attractive opportunities, but seeking potential gains always involves an element of risk. Among the most extreme categories on the risk-reward spectrum is speculating in futures—and stock index futures are no exceptions. In this chapter, however, an effort has been made to try to mitigate some of the risk facing the speculator in these futures. If the speculator uses the strategies suggested, there is no question that some—perhaps even many or most—of the trades made may end in losses, but the hope is that the strategies will enable the speculator to approach these futures markets intelligently and will offer a discipline that limits losses on losing trades while allowing profits on winning trades to run. The approaches suggested should be profitable in the long run, but no matter how reasonable or sophisticated the strategies may be, the risk is still present that the long run won't arrive until it's too late!

This chapter is reprinted from *Stock Index Futures*, Fabozzi & Kipnis (eds.), Dow Jones-Irwin, 1984. Used with permission.

Endnote

1   The author recognizes that he is taking some liberty by valuing the indices rather than the futures, but this practice eliminates the complications of theoretical time values appropriate to different settlement dates.

Chapter

18

Determining the Relevant Fair Value(s) of S&P 500 Futures

A fundamental consideration for potential users of stock index futures is the determination of the futures' break-even price or fair value. Conceptually, being able to sell futures at prices above the break-even, or to buy futures at prices below the break-even, offers opportunity for incremental gain. This chapter points out an important, though widely unappreciated, caveat. That is, no single break-even price is universally appropriate. Put another way, the break-even price for a given institution depends on the motivation of that firm as well as on its marginal funding and investing yield alternatives.

In this chapter, five differentiated objects are identified, and the calculations of the respective break-even futures prices are provided. The various objectives are: (1) to generate profits from arbitrage activities, (2) to create synthetic money market instruments, (3) to reduce exposure to equities, (4) to increase equity exposure, and (5) to maintain equity exposure using the most cost-effective instrument via stock/futures substitution. All these objectives have the same conceptual starting point, which relates to the fact that a combined long stock/short futures position generates a money market return composed of the dividends on the stock position as well as the basis[1] adjustment of the futures contract. Under the simplified assumptions of zero transactions costs and equal marginal borrowing and lending rates, the underlying spot/futures relationship can be expressed as follows:

$$F = S \left(1 + (i - d) \frac{t}{360} \right)$$

where: F = break-even futures price, S = spot index price, i = interest rate (expressed as a money market yield), d = projected dividend rate (expressed as a money market yield), and t = number of days from today's spot value date to the value date of the futures contract.

In equilibrium, the actual futures price equals the break-even futures price, and thus the market participant would either have no incentive to undertake the transactions or be indifferent between competing tactics for an equivalent goal.

Moving from the conceptual to the practical simply requires the selection of the appropriate marginal interest rate for the participant in question, as well as precise accounting for transactions costs. This chapter demonstrates that these considerations foster differences between the break-even prices among the alternative goals considered. Each goal is explained more fully, and the respective theoretical futures prices are presented.

Generating Profits from Arbitrage Activities

Generally, arbitrage is explained as a process whereby one identifies two distinct marketplaces where something is traded and then waits for opportunities to buy in one market at one price and sell in the other market at a higher price. This same process is at work for stock/futures arbitrage, but these market participants tend to view their activities with a slightly different slant. They enter an arbitrage trade whenever (a) buying stock and selling futures generates a return that exceeds financing costs, or (b) selling stocks and buying futures results in an effective yield (cost of borrowing) that falls below marginal lending rates. Completing arbitrages requires a reversal of the starting positions, and the cost for both buying and selling stocks and futures must be included in the calculations.[2] Thus, the total cost of an arbitrage trade reflects the bid/ask spreads on all the stocks involved in the arbitrage, the bid/ask spreads for all futures positions, and all commission charges on both stocks and futures.[3] Table 18-1 calculates these arbitrage costs under three different scenarios. In all cases, the current starting value of the stock portfolio, based on last-sale prices, is $100 million, and the S&P 500 index is valued at 335.00. The hedge ratio is calculated in the traditional manner.[4]

$$H = \frac{V \times \text{Beta}}{\text{S\&P} \times 500}$$

where: H = hedge ratio (number of futures contracts required), V = value of the portfolio, Beta = portfolio beta, and S&P = spot S&P 500 index price. The average price per share is estimated to be the S&P 500 index divided by five.

In column A, transactions are assumed to be costless, reflected by zero values for bid/ask spreads as well as zero commissions. In column B, more typical conditions are shown. Commissions on stock are assumed to be $.02 per share; bid/ask spreads on stocks are assumed to be 1/8 ($.125 per share); commissions on futures are assumed to be $12 on a round-turn basis (i.e., for both buy and sell transactions); and bid/ask spreads on futures are assumed to be 1 tick, or 0.05, worth $25.[5] Column C assumes the same commission structure as that of column B; but bid/ask spreads are somewhat higher, reflecting a decline in

Table 18–1: Arbitrage Break-evens

Arbitrage Costs	A	B	C
Index value	335	335	335
Size of portfolio	100,000,000	100,000,000	100,000,000
Average price per share	67	67	67
Number of shares	1,492,537	1,492,537	1,492,537
Commission per share of stock	0	0.02	0.02
Stock commissions per side	0	29,851	29,851
Stock commissions (RT)	0	59,701	59,701
Bid/ask per unit of stock	0	0.125	0.5
Bid/ask stock	0	186,567	746,269
Number of futures contracts	597	597	597
Commissions per round turn	0	12	12
Futures commissions	0	7164	7164
Bid/ask per futures contract	0.00	0.05	0.50
Bid/ask futures	0	14,925	149,250
Dollar costs	0	268,358	962,384
Index point cost	0.00	0.90	3.22
Marginal borrowing rate	9.00%	9.00%	9.00%
Marginal lending rate	8.00%	8.00%	8.00%
Dividend rate	3.50%	3.50%	3.50%
Shorter horizon (case a):			
Days to expiration	30	30	30
Upper Bound	336.54	337.43	339.76
Lower bound	336.26	335.36	333.03
No-arbitrage range	0.28	2.08	6.73
Longer horizon (case b):			
Days to expiration	60	60	60
Upper bound	338.07	338.97	341.29
Lower bound	337.51	336.61	334.29
No-arbitrage range	0.56	2.36	7.01

liquidity relative to the former case. This scenario might also be viewed as representing the case where impact costs of trying to execute a stock portfolio are expected to move initial bids or offers for a complete execution. The index point costs in all cases reflects the respective dollar costs on a per contract basis.

The arbitrageur would evaluate two independent arbitrage bounds: an upper bound and a lower bound. During those times when futures prices exceed the upper arbitrage boundary, profit could be made by financing the purchase of stocks at the marginal borrowing rate and selling futures. When the futures prices are below the lower bound, profits could be made by selling stocks and buying futures, thus creating a synthetic borrowing, and investing at the marginal lending rate. In both cases, the completed arbitrages would require an unwinding of all the original trades.

The upper bound is found by substituting the arbitrage firm's marginal borrowing rate in Eq. (1), and adding the arbitrage costs (in basis points) to this calculated value. In the case of the lower arbitrage boundary, the marginal lending rate is used for the variable i in Eq. (1), and the arbitrage costs are subtracted. The calculations in Table 18–1 assume marginal borrowing and lending rates of 9 percent and 8 percent, respectively, and a dividend rate of 3.5 percent. The upper and lower arbitrage boundaries are given for the three alternative cost structures. For comparative purposes, two sets of arbitrage boundaries are generated for two different terms.

Most obvious is the conclusion that an arbitrageur with a higher (lower) cost structure or a wider (narrower) differential between marginal borrowing and lending costs would face wider (narrower) no-arbitrage boundaries. In addition, Table 18–1 also demonstrates the time-sensitive nature of the difference between the two bounds, or the no-arbitrage range. As time to expiration expands, this range increases, monotonically, with all other considerations held constant.

Creating Synthetic Money Market Securities

The case of the firm seeking to construct a synthetic money market income security by buying stocks and selling futures is a slight variant of the arbitrage case described in the prior section.[6] In this situation, too, the firm seeks to realize a rate of return for the combined long stock/short futures positions; however, the relevant interest rate that underlies the determination of the break-even futures price is different. While the arbitrageur who buys stock and sells futures does so whenever the resulting gain betters his or her marginal borrowing rate, the synthetic fixed-income trader endeavors to outperform the marginal lending rate. For both, however, the imposition of transaction costs necessitates the sale of the futures at a higher price than would be dictated by the costless case.

Not surprisingly, the break-even price for this firm is directly related to both transaction costs and time to expiration. What may not be quite as readily apparent is the fact that, at least theoretically, situations may arise that provide no motivation for arbitrageurs to be sellers of futures, while at the same time offering a motivation for a potentially much larger audience of money managers to be futures sellers. Put another way, large-scale implementation of the synthetic money market strategy by many market investors could certainly enhance these firms' returns, but also have the more universally beneficial effect of reducing the range of futures price fluctuations that do not induce relative-price-based trading strategies.

Yet another seemingly perverse condition that is highlighted by these calculations is that firms that operate less aggressively in the cash market, and thereby tend to have lower marginal lending rates, are likely to have a greater incremental benefit from arranging synthetic securities than firms that seek out higher cash market returns. For example, assume firm A has access to Euro-deposit markets, while firm B deals only with lower-yielding U.S. domestic banks; assume further that the difference in marginal lending rates is .25 percent. Firm B's break-even futures price necessarily falls below that of firm A. At any point in time, however, the current futures bid is relevant for both firms. Assuming the two firms face the same transaction cost structures, this futures price would generate the same effective yield for the two firms. Invariably, firm B will find a greater number of yield enhancement opportunities than will firm A, and any time both firms are attracted to this strategy simultaneously, B's incremental gain will be greater.

Decreasing Equity Exposures

The case of the portfolio manager who owns equities and is looking to eliminate that exposure requires a further determination before the break-even calculation can be made. That is, two different break-evens would result, depending on whether the desired reduction in equity exposure is expected to be permanent or temporary.

First, consider the case where the shift out of equities is expected to be permanent. Hedging with futures simply defers the actual stock transaction. At the same time, it introduces futures transactions costs that would otherwise be saved if the immediate sale of stock were chosen. The determination of this break-even, therefore, requires an evaluation of the return that one could realize by liquidating stock today and investing the resulting funds in some money market security maturing at the futures value date, versus the return of hedging the stock portfolio today and subsequently liquidating it on the futures value date.

In calculating the returns from the traditional sell stocks/buy money market securities tactic, one should recognize that the liquidation cost effectively "haircuts" the portfolio. For example, the liquidation of a $100-million portfolio involves an immediate expense, so that some amount less than the original $100 million becomes available for reinvestment. Thus, the portfolio manager realizes a lower fixed-income return than the nominal yield on the proposed money market security. The break-even futures price would be that price that, when including all transactions costs, generates the same realized yield as the net money market return available from the shift into money market instruments.

In Table 18–2, the haircut is estimated to reflect half the bid/ask spread as well as the stock commissions. The same commission and bid/ask structure is assumed as that which faces the firms analyzed in the prior section; and, similarly, the same marginal investment rate (8 percent) is incorporated. Under these conditions, the manager who chooses the liquidation of the stock portfolio, and the investment of the proceeds at 8 percent (rather than hedging), realizes an effective net money market return of 6.51 percent for 30 days or 7.25 percent for 60 days. Respective break-even futures prices are 336.33 and 337.58.

The case where the decision to reduce exposure is more likely to be temporary involves a minor modification to the above calculations. That is, operating exclusively in the arena of stocks would add the cost of repurchasing a portfolio, thereby lowering the net money market return even further. In contrast, the hedging alternative generates no stock charges. As a consequence, the break-evens in this case are substantially below the break-evens required for the former example.

Increasing Equity Exposure

Perhaps the easiest situation to explain is the choice between buying today at the spot price versus buying in the future at the futures price. This determination simply requires calculating the forward value of the index, which, in turn, reflects the opportu-

Table 18–2:
Reducing Equity Exposures: Permanent Adjustment

Short hedging considerations:

Index value	335
Size of portfolio	100,000,000
Portfolio beta	1.0
Average price per share	67
Number of shares	1,492,537
Commission per share	0.02
Commissions per side	29,850.74
Bid/ask per stock	0.125
1/2 bid/ask stock	93,283.56
Total stock costs	123,134.30
Investable funds	99,876,865.70
Money market return	8.00%
Hedge calculation	597.0
Number of futures contracts	597
Commissions (rnd trn)	12.00
Futures commissions	7164.00
Bid/ask per contract	0.05
Bid/ask futures	14,925.00
Total futures costs	22,089.00
Total stock costs	123,134.30
Dollar costs/contract	243.26
Index point cost	0.49
Dividend rate	3.50%

Shorter horizon (case a):

Days to end point	30
Ending value	100,542,711.47
Net money market return	6.51%
Break-even futures price	336.33

Longer horizon (case b):

Days to end point	60
Ending value	101,208,557.24
Net money market return	7.25%
Break-even futures price	337.58

nity costs of foregoing interest income of a fixed-income investment alternative as well as an adjustment for transactions costs of futures, alone.[7] For the case of the same prototype firm discussed in the earlier sections and given the same portfolio, the opportunity cost is generated using the marginal lending rate of 8 percent. Thus, the portfolio manager would be indifferent between buying stocks now and hedging for a future purchase if the futures are cheaper than the price calculated from Eq. (1), inputting 8 percent for i. In this case, with the spot S&P 500 index at 335.00 and 30 days to the futures value date, the break-even price is 336.18. For a 60-day horizon, the break-even becomes 337.44.

Maintaining Equity Exposure in the Most Cost-Effective Instrument

Consider the case of the portfolio manager who currently holds equities with the existing degree of exposure at the desired level. Even this investor may find using futures to be attractive if they are sufficiently cheap. At some futures price it becomes attractive to sell the stocks and buy the futures, thereby maintaining the same equity exposure. The break-even price for this trader, then, would be the trigger price. That is, any lower futures price than this break-even would induce the substitution of futures for stocks and generate incremental benefits.

Like the prior case, this strategy rests on the comparison of present versus futures values, and again, the firms' marginal lending rate is the appropriate discounting factor. Regarding trading costs, commissions and bid/ask spreads for both stocks and futures must be taken into account, as the move from stocks to futures would be temporary. Thus, the break-even price would be lower than the zero-cost theoretical futures price by the basis point costs of the combined commissions and bid/ask spreads.

For the prototype firm with the marginal lending rate of 8 percent, under the same normal market assumptions used throughout, the break-even price for 30- and 60-day horizons becomes 335.36 and 336.61, respectively.[8]

Consolidation and Summary

Table 18–3 shows the respective break-even prices that are relevant to the various applications discussed in the chapter, in ascending order. All calculations relate to a firm with a marginal borrowing rate of 9 percent and a marginal lending rate of 8 percent. Break-even prices are given for two different time spans for the hedging period: 30 days and 60 days. Further,

Table 18–3:
Reducing Equity Exposures: Permanent Adjustment

	Days to Expiration	
	30-Days	60-Days
Lower arbitrage boundary[a]/futures substitution break-even	335.36	336.61
Temporary equity adjustment (short hedge) break-even	335.50	336.76
Long hedge break-even	336.18	337.44
Permanent equity adjustment (short hedge) break-even	336.33	337.58
Synthetic fixed income break-even	337.16	338.41
Upper arbitrage boundary	337.43	338.97

[a] Not reflective of costs associated with the uptick rule.

these calculations reflect the additional assumption of "normal" transactions cost and bid/ask spreads.

The highest price for which it becomes advantageous to take a long futures position is the long hedger's break-even price, and if prices decline sufficiently from this value so that they fall below the lower arbitrage boundary, additional market participants—namely arbitrageurs—will be induced to buy futures as well. The lowest price for which it becomes advantageous to sell futures would be the break-even for the temporary short hedger, and, in a similar fashion, if prices rise sufficiently above this level, additional short sellers will be attracted to these markets.

Note that regardless of the time horizon, the lowest price for which buying futures is justified (336.18 or 337.44) is higher than the highest price for which selling futures is justified (335.50 or 336.76). Thus, at every futures price, there is at least one market participant who "should" be using this market. Moreover, it is also interesting that if the futures price enables the arbitrageur to operate profitably, at least one other market participant would find the futures to be attractively priced as well. For example, if the futures are below the lower arbitrage bound, aside from the arbitrageur, the long-hedger would certainly be predisposed to buying futures rather than buying stocks, and, if the futures price is above the upper arbitrage bound, willing sellers would include arbitrageurs, both temporary and permanent short hedgers, and those constructing fixed-income securities.

The overall conclusion, then, is that it pays (literally) to evaluate the relevant break-even prices for any firm interested in any of the above strategies—a population that includes all firms that manage money market or equity portfolios. At every point in time, at least one strategy will dictate the use of futures as the preferred transactions vehicle because use of futures in the given situation will add incremental value. Failure to make this evaluation would undoubtedly result in either using futures at inopportune moments or, more likely, failing to use futures when it would be desirable to do so. In either case, neglecting to compare the currently available futures price to the correct break-even price ultimately results in suboptimal performance.

This chapter is reprinted from the *Journal of Futures Markets*, August 1991, published by John Wiley & Sons, Inc., © 1991.

The author appreciates helpful comments from Dan Siegel and two anonymous reviewers.

Endnotes

1 "Basis," in this chapter, is defined as the futures price minus the spot index value. Elsewhere, the calculation might be made with the two prices reversed.

2 If any fees or charges apply to the borrowing or lending mechanisms, these too would have to be incorporated in the calculations. Put another way, for the calculations that are presented in this chapter, the marginal borrowing and lending rates are effective rates, inclusive of all such fees.

3 Brennan and Schwaltz (1990) note that the cost of closing an arbitrage position may differ if the action is taken at expiration versus prior to expiration. Thus the appropriate arbitrage bound should reflect whether or not the arbitrageur is expecting (or hoping) to exercise an "early close-out option."

4 See Kawaller (1985) for a discussion of the justification for this hedge ratio.

5 In practice, it may be appropriate to assume two different cost structures for the upper- and lower-bound break-even calculations because costs differ depending on whether the

trade starts with long stock/short futures or vice versa. The difference arises because initiating the short stock/long futures arbitrage requires the sales of stock on an uptick. The "cost" of this requirement is uncertain because the transactions price is not known at the time the decision is made to enter the arbitrage. No analogous uncertainty exists when initiating the arbitrage in the opposite direction.

6   The case where the firm already holds the stock is considered later.

7   Stock costs would be roughly comparable whether one were to buy now or later, so they do not enter into the calculation. This treatment, admittedly, is not precise. For example, with a significant market move, the number of shares required may vary, as may the average bid-ask spreads; therefore, some differences may arise. Moreover, the statement ignores the fact that although absolute magnitudes may be identical in both the buy-now or buy-later cases, the present values of these charges may differ. This consideration, if taken into account more rigorously, would bias decision toward a later purchase. For the purposes of this analysis, however, these differences are ignored.

8   This result happens to be identical to that shown for the lower arbitrage bound of the firm operating with the same cost structure. As explained in footnote 5, however, the arbitrage firm that sells stock short has additional costs that do not apply to the stock/futures substituter. Thus, in practice, the break-even for the substituter is likely to be a higher price than the lower bound for the equivalent firm involved with arbitrage.

Bibliography

Brennan, M., and Schwartz, E. (1990): "Arbitrage in Stock Index Futures," *Journal of Business* 63:S7–S31.

Cornell, B., and French, K. (1983, Spring): "The Pricing of Stock Index Futures," *Journal of Futures Markets*, 3:1–14.

Figlewski, S. (1985, Summer): "Hedging with Stock Index Futures: Theory and Application in a New Market," *Journal of Futures Markets*, 5:183–199.

Hansen, N.H., and Kopprasch, R.W. (1984): "Pricing of Stock Index Futures," Fabozzi, F.J. and Kipnis, G.M. eds., *Stock Index Futures*, Dow Jones-Irwin, 6:65–79.

Kawaller, I.G. (1985, Fall): "A Comment on Figlewski's Hedging with Stock Index Futures: Theory and Application in a New Market," *Journal of Futures Markets*, 5:447–449.

Kawaller, I.G. (1987, June): "A Note: Debunking the Myth of the Risk-Free Return," *Journal of Futures Markets*, 7:327–331.

Chapter

19

Managing Cash Flow Risk in Stock Index Futures: The Tail Hedge

(with Timothy W. Koch)

T his chapter examines the use of the tail hedge as a means of managing cash flow risk associated with variation margin calls. A tail hedge involves taking a secondary position in the futures market to offset some of the original futures position. Traders take the opposite futures position with tails, expecting to generate gains that offset the financing costs of variation margin calls. Conversely, potential gains from cash inflows of variation margin would offset losses on the tail.[1]

Background

Speculators, hedgers, and arbitrageurs may follow different trading strategies, but all futures market participants face the same practical problem of uncertain cash flow obligations. Specifically, all bear the risk of intermittent cash outflows resulting from variation margin payments required because of adverse price movements of the futures position. At the very least, the cost of financing these dollar flows detracts from the profitability of the futures position. At worst, the cash flow obligation could force premature liquidation and seriously disrupt a well-considered hedging or trading strategy.

Fielitz and Gay (1986) recently developed a model that portfolio managers can use to establish liquidity reserves against such potential cash outflows. The model determines the amount of funds to be held in reserve given the portfolio's size, its systematic risk (beta), the investment term, and management's assessment of an acceptable probability of exhausting the liquidity reserve.

One problem with this approach, however, is that the liquidity reserve is potentially large. In one example, the target reserve equaled 13.8 percent of the total portfolio to provide a 99-percent probability that the fund could handle margin calls over a 20-day period. If the investment term were doubled to 40 days, say, the required liquidity reserve would increase to 19.6 percent, which amounts to $9.8 million for a $50-million equity portfolio.

Such a liquidity reserve effectively increases the capital requirements for transacting in futures by not a trivial amount. Moreover, because the reserve would probably consist of highly marketable securities, such as federal funds and Treasury bills, investment in qualifying instruments may alter a firm's desired portfolio risk and return profile. The tail hedge is an alternative means of dealing with this reserve problem.

The Institutional Mechanics of Tail Hedges

Futures transactions entail cash flow risk associated with variation margin requirements. Whenever futures prices move against the initial futures position, a trader or hedger must pay cash equal to the change in value of the position to cover the loss.[2] However the payment is financed, the margin requirement imposes both explicit costs that reduce the effective return and implicit costs that the increased monitoring entails. Establishing a liquidity reserve is one approach to handling margin calls, as Fielitz and Gay recommend.

An alternative method of managing this risk is to establish a tail, or underhedge position. The tail is a smaller futures position that offsets a small fraction of the initial futures trade. For example, a trader long 200 contracts without tailing might take a coincident short position in five of the same futures contracts. Ideally, the interest cost of variation margin financing on the long position, should the futures price decline, would be offset by gains on the tail. If a trader is short futures initially, a tail calls for a smaller, long offset.

Operationally, the cash flow requirements can be satisfied by establishing a trilateral arrangement among the customer (trader), the futures broker, and the bank that handles the cash flows. The arrangement consists of an open line of credit, allowing the customer to take down funds as required, and a companion interest-bearing deposit account. The bank lends the customer funds when margin calls require cash infusions and invests excess margin balances when they occur.[3]

Loans of this type generally require a demand note that stipulates the maximum amount of available funds, a security agreement that establishes a lender's lien on assets used as collateral, and the assignment of a hedge account that attaches funds in the brokerage account as collateral. Within this framework, the broker contacts the bank directly when additional margin financing is needed, and the bank increases the customer's loan. When prices move favorably and excess margin exists, the bank withdraws the excess to pay down the loan or deposits it in an interest-bearing account. Such an arrangement satisfies liquidity concerns, but does not alleviate the risk associated with unknown financing costs.

Determining the Size
of the Tail Hedge

The purpose of a tail hedge is to offset the interest cost associated with financing the line of credit in support of margin calls. The tail should be constructed so that the change in value of financing the futures variation margin is exactly offset by the change in value of the tail position:

$$\text{(i) } (d/360) \text{ (FP) } N = -(FP)n, \qquad (1)$$

where: i = the assumed annual interest rate applied to the variation margin payment or receipt;

d = the number of days remaining until settlement of the variation margin financing or investment;

FP = change in value of a single futures contract;

N = the number of contracts in the initial futures position; and

n = the number of contracts in the tail position.

The negative sign indicates that the tail position is opposite in form (short versus long) to the initial futures position. The size of the tail implied by equation (1) reduces to:

$$n = -(i) \, (d/360)N. \qquad (2)$$

Equation (2) derives from the fact that, when multiplied by the change in the value of a single futures contract, the term on the left equals the expected profit (loss) on the tail, and the term on the right equals the expected interest payment (return) on the variation margin financing (investment). In other words, the tail hedge tries to equate the present value of interest flows on variation margin activity with the present value of gains or losses on the tail. A liquidity reserve, in contrast, imposes an up-front cost that far exceeds the present value cost of variation margin payments.

One difficulty in applying equation (2) arises because of uncertainty regarding the relevant interest rate and the natural drift in d as expiration of the futures contract approaches. Two factors complicate the choice of interest rate. First, financing rates applicable when the margin is deficient typically exceed investment yields when surplus margin exists. Because the tail hedger does not know the direction of futures prices over the hedge period, neither rate is better *ex ante*. Second, variation margin requirements normally are handled daily, so a different interest rate applies each successive day, unless the yield curve remains flat throughout the holding period and the futures price moves consistently for or against the hedger.[4]

Finally, even if managers knew which interest rate applied, expected interest payments decrease toward expiration date as d approaches zero. Appropriate risk management thus requires that portfolio managers periodically recalculate the size of the tail to ensure that it offsets the interest obligation from variation margin. Because these problems cannot be eliminated, the final tail results will only approximately offset the costs or benefits of variation margin flows.

An Illustration

Consider the problems faced by an equity portfolio manager who decides to hedge $25 million in equities. The equities exhibit a beta equal to 1.0. The manager is concerned that stock prices will decline over the next six months and thus decides to use the S&P 500 futures contract to hedge.[5] At the time of the decision, the S&P 500 futures contract is priced at 205, with 150 days remaining to expiration, and the S&P 500 index is trading at 200. In this instance, the correct base hedge would require selling 250 futures contracts ($25 million/[(200)×(500]) = 250).

If the hedge were to be maintained until the futures expiration date, the manager would expect to earn an amount equal to the reinvested value of the dividends paid on the equities over the next 150 days plus the basis adjustment.[6] The dollar value of the basis adjustment equals the product of the basis (the futures price minus the spot index value), the number of contracts in the hedge, and the multiplier of 500. In this case the dollar amount is $625,000.

Before establishing a tail hedge, the manager must determine the term to settlement day for all variation financing or investing and the relevant interest rate. Typically, the term of the hedge is set equal to the number of days until the original futures position is expected to be closed, but, in fact, any subsequent day could be used. Similarly, the interest rate is set at the term rate available over the same interval, assuming that the yield curve will remain flat during the holding period.

A 10-percent interest rate in this example, with a term of 150 days, requires a tail hedge of ten contracts:

$$n = -250(0.10)(150/360) = -10.4$$

If the base hedge is 250 short contracts, the tail requires ten long contracts, as contracts are only traded in unit increments. The net position, therefore, would be 240 short contracts. Table 19–1 demonstrates the recalculation of the tail every 15 days. It assumes that even though the period for financing or investing decreases every day, the appropriate financing rate remains at 10 percent. Table 19–2 shows the resulting variation margin changes on the base positions and corresponding offsets generated by the tail under a scenario assuming a rising futures price. The table also assumes that futures prices increase by 250 basis points (2.50 index points) immediately following the adjustment to the tail.[7] Note that the actual tail reflects a rounding of the

Table 19–1: Calculating the Tail

Days Remaining in Hedge Period (d)	Tail Calculation [n = –250(0.1)(d/360)]
150	10.4 ~ 10
135	9.4 ~ 9
120	8.3 ~ 8
105	7.3 ~ 7
90	6.3 ~ 6
75	5.2 ~ 5
60	4.2 ~ 4
45	3.1 ~ 3
30	2.1 ~ 2
15	1.0 ~ 1
0	0 ~ 0

Table 19–2: Simulation

Days Remaining in Hedge	S&P Futures Price	Variation Margin	Interest on Variation Margin[a]	Number of Contracts in Tail[b]	Tail Profit[c]
150	207.50	$312,500	$13,021	10	$12,500
135	210.00	312,500	11,719	9	11,250
120	212.50	312,500	10,417	8	10,000
105	215.00	312,500	9,115	7	8,750
90	217.50	312,500	7,813	6	7,500
75	220.00	312,500	6,510	5	6,250
60	222.50	312,500	5,208	4	5,000
45	225.00	312,500	3,906	3	3,750
30	227.50	312,500	2,604	2	2,500
15	230.00	312,500	1,302	1	1,250
0	232.50	312,500	0	0	0
Cumulative results		$3,437,500	$71,615		$68,750

[a] Variation margin × 10 percent × days remaining/360
[b] 250 × 10 percent × days remaining/360; rounded to nearest integer.
[c] Tail position × 2.50 × $500.

calculated value for n, as contracts must be bought or sold in whole units. In this example the rounding consistently caused a somewhat smaller tail than that stipulated by the equation.

At the outset, the objective was to earn the dividends from owning the stocks plus the basis adjustment, where this latter component equals five index points per contract ($625,000) for the base hedge. In this example, the expected outcome is not achieved precisely. In the scenario presented, the original equities appreciate by $4,062,500, reflecting an 18.75 percent increase in the S&P 500 index. The hedge, however, produces a consolidated loss of $3,440,365 made up of a) the base variation margin ($3,437,500), b) its associated finance charges ($71,615), and c) the tail profits ($68,750), which serve to reduce overall hedge losses.

The net result is that the hedger earns $622,135 plus dividends. The tailed hedge position actually earns $2,865 less than the target established when the hedge was initiated. This is a mismatch of less than 0.5 percent of the expected basis adjustment. What is most important, however, is that the earnings would have been $71,615 less, or a mismatch of more than 11 percent of that target without the tail.

Suppose instead that the S&P 500 futures price were to decrease by 250 basis points every 15 days. Interest on variation margin would then represent income exactly equal to the amount in Table 19–2, and the tail position would produce losses. In this case the spot index and futures prices would settle at 177.50, and the loss in equity value would equal $2,812,500. The hedge position, inclusive of interest income less tail losses, would produce a gain of $3,440,365, for aggregate earnings of $627,865, or $2,865 above the target.

As is true for most hedges, it is difficult to execute the tail hedge with the precision demonstrated in Table 19–2. The biggest challenge is to match the correct number of base futures contracts with the underlying equities. Any discrepancy, or any missed estimate of n, affects the tail hedge results. Still, the tail hedge clearly reduces the variance of expected returns around the target.

Conclusion

Variation margin requirements on stock index futures transactions increase the cash flow risk that portfolio managers face. Rather than establish a liquidity reserve from which funds can be withdrawn to meet payment obligations, the manager may want to follow an alternative procedure that uses tail hedges. The tail hedge requires a smaller up-front investment and does not alter a firm's risk and return profile.

This copyrighted material is reprinted from the *Journal of Portfolio Management* (Fall 1988), with permission from Institutional Investor, Inc.

Endnotes

1 When futures prices change favorably, traders can withdraw and invest the excess variation margin. The use of a tail hedge eliminates this potential benefit. Firms that establish separate liquidity reserves gain directly from cash inflows associated with their variation margin position.

2 Collins and Fabozzi (1989) describe the mechanics of and institutional requirements underlying variation margin rules.

3 Such lending arrangements are common in the case of agriculture hedge loans to finance initial margin, maintenance margin, and brokerage commissions arising from trading futures contracts. See "Risk Management Guide for Ag Lenders," by the Chicago Mercantile Exchange.

4   It is possible that changes in the level of rates can be offset exactly by changes in rates associated with movements along the yield curve.

5   A beta of 1.0 indicates that changes in the value of the firm's equity portfolio exactly match percentage movements on the S&P 500 index. A portfolio beta different from 1.0 affects the number of contracts that should be used to hedge the initial equity exposure. See Fabozzi and Peters (1989).

6   The target earnings need to be adjusted whenever the projected hedge period ends prior to expiration of the futures contract. The incomplete basis adjustment reduces target earnings by a factor equal to the theoretical basis anticipated at the end of the hedge period.

7   This is the worst possible timing sequence of price changes.

References

Collins, B., and F. Fabozzi. "Mechanics of Trading Stock Index Futures." Chapter 5 in the *Handbook of Stock Index Futures and Options*, F. Fabozzi and G. Kipnis, eds. Homewood, IL: Dow Jones-Irwin, 1989.

Fabozzi, F., and E. Peters. "Hedging with Stock Index Futures." Chapter 13 in the *Handbook of Stock Index Futures and Options*, F. Fabozzi and G. Kipnis, eds. Homewood. IL: Dow Jones-Irwin, 1989.

Fielitz, B., and G. Gay. "Managing Cash Flow Risks in Stock Index Futures." *Journal of Portfolio Management*, 74-76 (Winter 1986).

Kawaller, I. "Going the Extra Mile." *Journal of Cash Management* (July/August 1986).

"Risk Management Guide for Ag Lenders." Chicago: Chicago Mercantile Exchange, 1985.

Chapter

20

The Relationship Between the S&P 500 Index and the S&P 500 Index Futures Prices

(with Paul D. Koch
and Timothy W. Koch)

T he advent of markets for stock index futures and options has profoundly changed the nature of trading on stock exchanges. These markets offer investors flexibility in altering the composition of their portfolios and in timing their transactions. Futures and options markets also provide opportunities to hedge the risks involved with holding diversified equity portfolios. As a consequence, significant portions of cash market equity transactions are now tied to futures and options market activity.

The effect of the stock index futures and options markets on traditional stock trading has aroused both the ire of critics and the acclaim of supporters. Critics allege that futures trading unduly influences the underlying equity markets, especially on days when futures contracts expire. For example, on various expiration days from 1984 to 1985, the stock markets closed with equity prices either rising or falling dramatically during the final hour of trading.[1] The phenomenon of sharp price swings and the seeming relation to futures market activity has, especially in the wake of the October 19, 1987, stock market crash, prompted various suggestions for modifying the design of the contracts to lessen their impact on the market.

Proponents of futures markets, on the other hand, do not view the final-day price swings as a problem, since the swings are generally temporary and nonsystematic. In fact, proponents argue that such markets provide an important price discovery function and offer an alternative marketplace for adjusting equity exposure.

This chapter addresses some basic questions that have a fundamental bearing on the debate between the critics and advocates of futures markets. Do intra-day movements in the index futures price provide predictive information about subsequent movements in the index, or do movements in the index presage futures price changes? Is the price relationship different on expiration days and the days leading up to expiration?

Analysis of the Standard and Poor's (S&P) 500 futures and the S&P 500 index can help answer these questions. This chapter shows that lags exist not only between movements in futures prices and subsequent movements in the index, but also between the index and subsequent futures prices, though these lags are not symmetrical. The index lags behind the futures price by up to 45 minutes, but the futures price tends to trail the index only briefly. Examination of the lagged relationships on expiration days and the days prior to them indicates that the relationships are remarkably stable, implying that neither expiration day volatility nor the climate preceding these days interferes with the price discovery function that index futures seem to offer.[2]

An Overview of the S&P 500 Index and Index Futures

The S&P 500 stock index represents the market value of all outstanding common shares of 500 firms selected by Standard and Poor's. An S&P 500 futures contract represents the purchase or sale of a hypothetical basket of the 500 stocks underlying the S&P 500 index, set in a proportion consistent with the weights set by the index, with a market value equal to the futures price times a multiplier of 500. The futures price should be tied to the cost of investing in and carrying an S&P 500 look-alike basket of stocks until the expiration of the index future. The cost of carry incorporates transactions fees, taxes, and the expense of financing the investment, minus the dividends derived from the basket of stocks and any additional reinvestment income.

As a requirement for gaining access to the market, traders must post an initial margin deposit or collateral equal to a fraction of the futures contract market value (price × 500). Futures prices change virtually continuously throughout each trading day, and at day's end traders must cover any losses when prices move against them. Alternatively, they may withdraw any profit in excess of their performance bond requirement should prices move favorably. During the period from which data for this study were drawn, contracts expired on the third Fridays of March, June, September, and December, with the futures contracts marked to the closing index value at 4:15 p.m., Eastern time.[3]

Basic Functions of Stock Index Futures

Stock index futures typically serve three functions: trading, hedging, and arbitrage. First, traders can take speculative positions in futures to take advantage of anticipated broad market price movements. Second, hedging, which involves the purchase or sale of index futures in anticipation of an intended cash market trade, compensates for adverse price moves in the cash market, and thus reduces aggregate risk. Simple hedges typically involve the purchase (sale) of an asset in the cash market and sale (purchase) of futures contracts on the same asset. As long as the cash-futures spread remains the same and the costs of effecting and financing the transaction are covered, gains (losses) on the cash market purchase are countered by losses (gains) on the future. The investor thus may mitigate the risk of loss and the possibility of gain on the cash market purchase.

Arbitrage is a third strategy served by stock index futures. It involves the simultaneous purchase and sale of stocks and futures and subsequently enables an investor to capture profits from realignments of relative prices following an apparent inconsistency in the index and the index futures price. When the index futures price moves outside the range determined by the cost of the look-alike basket and the cost of carry, arbitrage will tend to drive the futures price and the index toward their cost-of-carry relationship. If the actual futures price is higher than the cost of the look-alike basket and the cost of carry, the futures contract is overvalued, justifying the purchase of the look-alike basket of stocks and the simultaneous sale of the futures contract. If the futures price falls below the price of the look-alike portfolio plus the cost of carry, the futures contract is undervalued, and the reverse trade would be profitable. In both cases, the arbitrage transactions realign the futures price and the index.

Because physical delivery does not take place, the futures contract is said to be "settled in cash." Cash settlement is an important feature of stock index futures. An arbitrageur who has sold futures and bought the underlying basket of stocks does not deliver the basket of stocks to the investor who bought futures. Instead the arbitrageur must sell the basket of stocks. Any open futures positions are marked to the final settlement index calculation when the futures expire. Once the arbitrageur pays or receives the value of the price change from the prior day, the position is closed. A common practice for arbitrageurs, however, is to trade large blocks of stocks or whole portfolios at prices tied to closing prices on the futures expiration days. As a result, these large volumes of orders late in the day have tended, on some occasions, to create at least temporary imbalances in the cash equity markets.

Movements in Futures Prices

Numerous studies have explained the price relationship between stock index futures and the underlying stocks in terms of arbitrage behavior. Futures prices normally vary relative to stock prices within ranges that are not sufficient to trigger arbitrage. In fact, arbitrage opportunities are often not available. A number of scholars have attempted to identify and measure arbitrage trading boundaries.[4] Their results indicate that the futures to cash price differential, referred to as the "basis," should fall within boundaries determined by the cost of carry. Because market interest rates have historically exceeded the dividend rate on common stocks, the "fair value" or theoretical stock index futures price normally exceeds the stock index.[5]

Conventional wisdom among professional traders dictates that movements in the S&P 500 futures price affect market expectations of subsequent movements in cash prices. The futures price presumably embodies all available information regarding events that will affect cash prices. Purchase or sale of index futures requires one transaction, while purchase or sale of a look-alike portfolio generally involves 200 or more stocks and a minimum $5 million investment. Consequently, the futures price is likely to respond to new information more quickly than cash market prices in general and thus more quickly than the S&P 500 index. This lag of the index behind the futures price results because the underlying stocks must be traded in order for the index to reflect a change in value. Since most index stocks do not trade each minute, the cash market responds to the new information with a lag.[6]

S&P 500 index movements may similarly convey information about subsequent price variation in the futures contract. However, the lag of the futures price behind the index is likely to be much shorter than the lag of the index behind the futures price. Futures traders are likely to incorporate recent changes in the index in their pricing decisions. For example, if the index declines because investors are selling stocks connected with options trading, the decline may induce a change in sentiment that is reflected in subsequent futures prices.

Tests of the Intra-Day Relationship between S&P 500 Futures and the S&P 500 Index

In fact, a complex set of potential relationships could exist between S&P 500 futures and the S&P 500 index prices. Movements in each are thought to be influenced by the past and current movements of both as well as by other market information. The study reported on in this chapter tried to gauge the magnitude and variability of the relationships between the index and the futures by estimating distributed lags between the two prices. Distributed lags employ a method of weighting past data to determine their effects on the data under study.

The pattern of lags between futures and the index may not be constant over time. While shifting patterns are conceivable throughout the life of the futures contract, the focus of interest on expiration day effects begs the question of whether these temporal relationships show any differentiation on those days. On expiration days, the traders' need to close positions may generate market imbalances that could conceivably overwhelm the mechanism by which new information influences index futures and cash market prices. An expiration-day breakdown in this mechanism would diminish the benefits of the futures market—at least on expiration day—as a medium for discovery.

The data are minute-by-minute prices of index futures contracts and the S&P 500 index on all trading days in 1984 and 1985. The Chicago Mercantile Exchange provided the data.[7] Pairing the reported index with the last index futures price quoted during the minute that the index appeared yielded 360 pairs of index and futures observations each day (six-hour trading day × 60 observations per hour). To judge whether the index futures-index relationship changes as the expiration day approaches, lags were estimated for six trading days in each quarter, beginning in the second quarter of 1984 and ending with the last quarter of 1985.[8] The days are 88, 60, 30, and 14 days prior to expiration, 1 day prior to expiration, and expiration day. These days were chosen to represent the approach of expiration and the effect of this approach on the index futures-index relationship.

The nature and extent of the lead/lag relationships between index futures prices and the index were measured using a number of analyses. First, a time series analysis was performed to study the movements of futures prices relative to prior futures prices. Next, the same method of analysis gauged movement of the S&P 500 index based on past index performance. These time series analyses studied the minute-to-minute changes in both the index and the futures prices. The next step in the analysis was to construct a model to describe the dynamic intra-day price relationships between the index and the futures prices. In this model, index movements depend on their own past movements, current and past movements in the futures price, and other relevant market information. Likewise, futures price movements are modeled to depend on their own past movements, current and past movements in the index, and other relevant market information.[9]

Consistent evidence on both the form of the lag relationships and their stability over time emerges from these tests: first, the contemporaneous relationship between futures prices and the index is quite strong—dwarfing the lagged relationships. In fact, the futures and index move almost in lock step. Second, lags between futures prices and the index are not symmetrical. The index lags behind the futures price by up to 45 minutes, while the futures price lags behind the index only briefly if at all. This result supports the contention that futures do, in fact, serve a price discovery function. Third, the lagged relationships do not appreciably change as expiration day approaches or on expiration day itself.

Different patterns of lagged relationships between S&P 500 futures and the S&P 500 index are given in Figure 20–1. It shows the distributed lag coefficients for two days in the fourth quarter of 1984; results for other days in this contract period, as well as days in other contract periods, are quite similar. Typically, the first coefficient, which describes the contemporaneous relationship, is the greatest, or one of the greatest, on each day. In the panels showing lags from futures to the index, relatively large and statistically significant coefficients show up with lags as long as 45 minutes. Panels showing lags from the index to futures typically show the one-minute lag as the largest coefficient and the only one that is significant. These results parallel evidence garnered from earlier time-series analyses.[10]

Figure 20–1 also shows quite similar patterns in the distributed lag coefficients 88 days prior to expiration day and on expiration day. Coefficients showing the lead from futures to the index continue to be mostly positive even on expiration day. They are significant or nearly significant through 20 to 30 minutes on each day, though the lag appears somewhat less on expiration day. Other quarters record quite similar patterns.

Implications

Evidence uncovered in the tests of lagged relationships between S&P 500 futures prices and the S&P 500 index points to the usefulness of the futures as a predictor of broad equity market movements measured by the index. The S&P 500 futures price and underlying index evidently respond to market information simultaneously, and the index shows lags of up to 45 minutes behind the futures. Importantly, the magnitudes of the contemporaneous effects on different days are consistently much larger than the lagged effects. Thus, though the price discovery function has been demonstrated, the indications of forthcoming cash

Figure 20–1: Sample Distributed Lags for the S&P 500 Index and S&P 500 Index Futures Prices

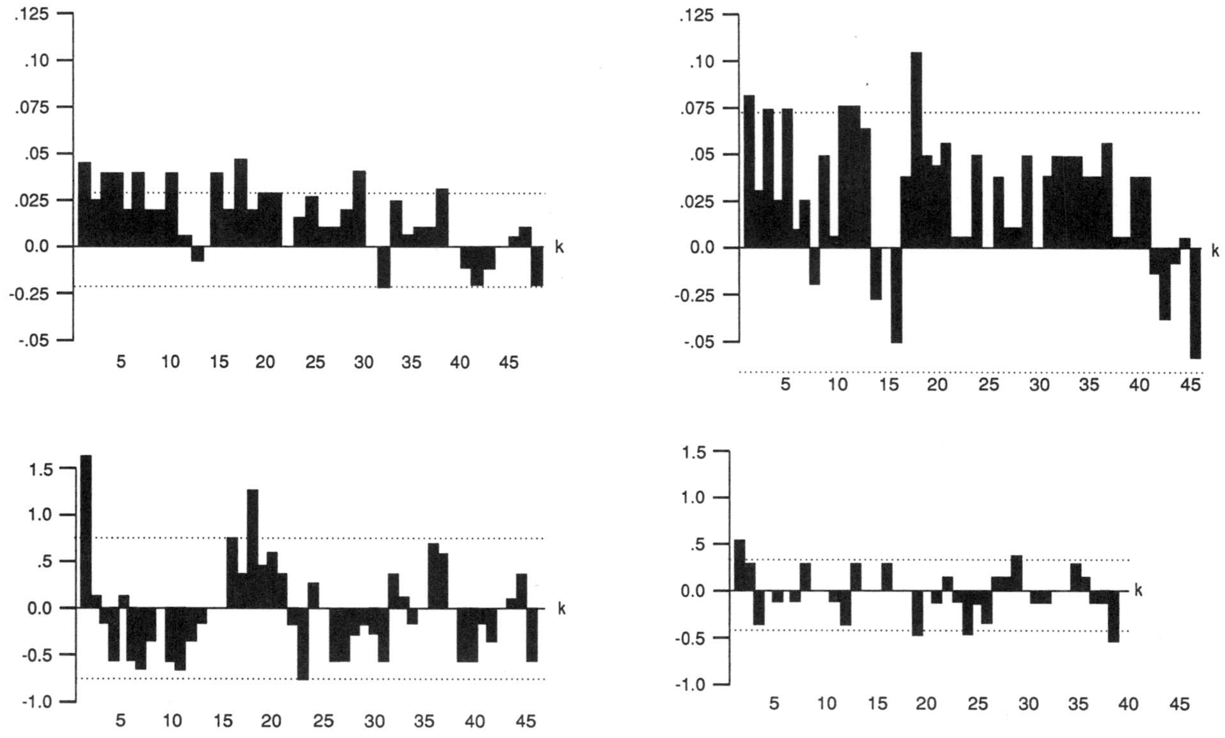

09/24/84: 88 days prior to expiration

12/21/84: expiration day

Figure 20–1 shows the relationship between minute-to-minute movements in the S&P 500 futures price and the S&P 500 Index. The top graph in each set shows how past minute-to-minute movements in the futures price affect current movements in the index, and the bottom figure shows how past movements in the index affect current movements in the futures price.

The vertical axis in each figure represents the magnitude of the minute-to-minute impacts of each value on the other. The horizontal axis charts the number of minute-to-minute lags incorporated into the model. For example, for $k = 1$ minute lag, the value plotted in the top graph shows the impact of the futures price change one minute earlier on the current index value. At the number "20" on the horizontal axis, the effect on the current index value of the futures price 20 minutes earlier is plotted.

When the vertical lines within the graph fall between the two dotted horizontal lines, the magnitude of the distributed lag coefficient is less than twice its standard error, and thus is not statistically significant. When the vertical lines within the graph fall outside the dotted lines, the magnitude of the distributed lag coefficient is more than twice its standard error, and, thus, is statistically significant.

When the vertical lines are concentrated in the positive portion of the figure (above 0.0), most of the lagged impacts of one price on the other are positive, that is, increases in one price are then followed by increases in the other price.

When the vertical lines are concentrated in the negative portion of the figure (below 0.0), most of the lagged impacts of one price on the other are negative, that is, increases in one price are then followed by decreases in the other.

market changes provided by past futures prices are not sufficient to provide an exploitable trading strategy.

Consistency in the lagged relationships over the days approaching expiration day and on expiration day also indicates that the pattern of lags between futures and the index is not disturbed by the closing out of arbitrage positions. This consistency implies that futures trading continues to make its contribution to price discovery, even on expiration days that transpired without market activity restrictions.

This chapter is reprinted from Federal Reserve Bank of Atlanta *Economic Review* 73 (May/June 1988):2-10.

Endnotes

1   The term "triple witching hour" was used to describe this trading period because the Chicago Mercantile Exchange's (CME) S&P 500 futures, the Chicago Board of Trade Options Exchange's (CBOE) S&P 100 options, and contracts on individual stock options all expired on the third Fridays of March, June, September, and December. After March 1987, the final day of trading for S&P 500 futures was moved to the day prior.

2   These results do not explain expiration day swings, nor do they suggest that such swings are desirable.

3   Since this study, the final settlement procedures for S&P 500 futures have changed. Contracts currently expire one business day prior to the third Friday of the contract month, with the final settlement price based on a special calculation of the Friday opening prices for each of the 500 stocks. Upon expiration, one final cash adjustment is made to reflect the last day's gains or losses.

4   Cornell and French (1983a, b); Figlewski (1984a, b); Modest and Sundaresan (1983); and Stoll and Whaley (1986).

5   The theoretical upper and lower bounds are discussed extensively in the literature. For example, see Stoll and Whaley (1986): 8-10, or Kawaller (1987): 447-49.

6   New information could affect a subset of index stocks disproportionately relative to the entire stock market. In such cases, not all index stocks must be traded each minute for the index to adjust completely and quickly to new information.

7   At the time of this study, the index was available only each minute. Since then, index quotations have been calculated and disseminated at about 15-second intervals.

8   This chapter's sample is restricted to the last three contracts in 1984 and all contracts that expired in 1985. Also note that futures trade for 15 minutes after the stock markets close. Quotes from these 15 minutes are not considered in this analysis. Finally, since September 30, 1985, quotes are available beginning at 8:30 A.M., but the analysis is restricted to the six hours (360 observations) from 9:01 A.M. and 3:00 P.M. so that the results can be compared across quarters.

9   In the context of this model, zero restrictions are tested on the distributed lag coefficients, allowing, alternately, the contemporaneous coefficient and the coefficient at lag one minute to remain unconstrained. See Kawaller, Koch, and Koch (1987) for details.

10 The tests with no restrictions on the contemporaneous and first coefficients also confirm the longer lags from the futures to the index and the very short lag from the index to the futures.

Bibliography

Cornell, B. and French, K. "The Pricing of Stock Index Futures." *Journal of Futures Markets* 3: 1-14 (Summer 1983a).

_____, and _____. "Taxes and the Pricing of Stock Index Futures." *Journal of Finance* 38: 675-94 (June 1983b).

Elton, Edwin J., Gruber, Martin J., and Rentzler, Joel. "Intra-day Tests of the Efficiency of the Treasury Bill Futures Market." *Review of Economics and Statistics* 66: 129-37 (February 1984).

Figlewski, Stephen. "Explaining the Early Discounts on Stock Index Futures: The Case for Disequilibrium." *Financial Analysts Journal* 40: 43-47 (July-August 1984a).

_____. "Hedging Performance and Basis Risk in Stock Index Futures." *Journal of Finance* 39:657-69 (July 1984b).

_____. "Hedging with Stock Index Futures: Theory and Application in a New Market." *Journal of Futures Markets* 5: 183-99 (Summer 1985).

Gastineau, Gary, and Madansky, Albert. "S&P 500 Stock Index Futures Evaluation Tables." *Financial Analysts Journal* 39: 68-76 (November-December 1983).

Geweke, John. "Testing the Exogeneity Specification in the Complete Dynamic Simultaneous Equations Model." *Journal of Econometrics* 6: 163-85 (April 1978).

Granger, Clive W. "Investigating Causal Relations by Econometric Models and Cross-Spectral Methods." *Econometrics* 37: 423-38 (July 1969).

Haugh, Larry D. "Checking the Independence of Two Covariance-Stationary Time Series: A Univariate Residual Cross-Correlation Approach." *Journal of the American Statistical Association* 71: 378-85 (June 1976).

Kawaller, Ira G. "A Comment on Figlewski's 'Hedging with Stock Index Futures: Theory and Application in a New Market.'" *Journal of Futures Markets* 5: 447-49 (Fall 1985).

_____. "A Note: Debunking the Myth of the Risk-Free Return." *Journal of Futures Markets* 7: 327-31 (June 1987).

_____, Koch, Paul D., and Koch, Timothy W. "The Temporal Price Relationship between S&P 500 Futures Prices and the S&P 500 Index." *Journal of Finance* 5: 1309-29 (December 1987).

Koch, Paul D., and Ragan, James F., Jr. "Investigating the Causal Relationship Between Wages and Quits: An Exercise in Comparative Dynamics." *Economic Inquiry* 24: 61-83 (January 1986).

Koch, Paul D., and Yang, Shie-Shien. "A Method for Testing the Independence of Two Time Series that Accounts for a Potential Pattern in the Cross-Correlation Function." *Journal of the American Statistical Association* 81: 533-44 (June 1986).

Modest, David, and Sundaresan, Mahadeaum. "The Relationship between Spot and Futures Prices in Stock Index Futures Markets: Some Preliminary Evidence." *Journal of Futures Markets* 3: 15-41 (Summer 1983).

Stoll, Hans R., and Whaley, Robert E. "Expiration Day Effects of Index Options and Futures." Vanderbilt University, March 1986.

U.S. Securities and Exchange Commission. Letter to the Honorable John D. Dingell, June 13, 1986a.

_____. Letter to Mr. Kenneth J. Leiber and others, June 13, 1986b.

_____. *Roundtable on Index Arbitrage,* July 9, 1986c.

Chapter

21

Applications of Nikkei Stock Index Futures and Options

The institutional use of Nikkei futures and options undoubtedly will parallel applications for domestic derivatives such as the S&P 500 futures. Thus, we may expect Nikkei futures and options instruments to be applied to stock/futures arbitrage, construction of synthetic money market investments, portfolio insurance, tactical asset allocation or just plain hedging and speculation. Whatever the overall strategy, ultimately Nikkei futures and options will be used to either increase or decrease exposure to Japanese equity markets. They do so in a way that creates some interesting opportunities—especially for the investor/manager with a dollar-denominated portfolio.

Increasing Exposure to Japanese Equities

Consider the U.S. manager who enters the Japanese stock market because he believes the Nikkei average will move higher, and he wants to participate in the growth. In fact, by buying stocks, two exposures are realized: (a) a pure stock exposure and (b) a currency exposure. In other words, profits or losses will depend on both the movement of the stock prices (i.e., whether the Nikkei Stock Average rises or falls) and the strength of yen relative to dollars. Conceivably, the yen-denominated value of the stocks could rise, but the dollar value could fall because the effect of the weakening yen could override the appreciation of the stocks.[1]

If you want to eliminate this problem altogether, the CME's Nikkei futures and options will likely be the instruments of choice. With these contracts, gains or losses are based solely on the movement of the Nikkei Average with no sensitivity to the level of the dollar/yen exchange rate. To increase exposure to Japanese equities, one could execute a long futures trade, long calls, or short puts. A long futures position establishes an exposure with both unlimited profit potential and unlimited risk; long calls offer unlimited profit with limited risk (for a cost); and short puts provide limited profit opportunity but unlimited risk in a down market. The choice is a matter of business judgment and should be based on a market outlook, the investors capacity for risk and his objectives and philosophy.

Table 21-1 demonstrates this case. It assumes that at the start (T0), the investor is looking to establish a position in Japanese equities originally worth $7 million. The theoretical hedge ratio for the Nikkei futures is calculated as follows:

$$H = \frac{Value}{NKS \times \$5/Spot} \cdot Beta$$

where H   =   # of long futures contracts required
      Value =   portfolio value (in yen)
      NKS   =   price of the Nikkei Stock Average
      $5   =   the futures multiplier
      Spot   =   spot exchange rate (American terms)
      Beta   =   the portfolio's beta (relative to the Nikkei Stock Average)

Table 21–1:
Static Nikkei Futures/No Currency Futures

	T0	T1	T2	T3
Nikkei Price Index	35,000	35,500	36,000	36,500
Nikkei Futures Price	35,000	35,500	36,000	36,500
Spot yen prices ($/100 yen)	0.7500	0.7300	0.7100	0.6900
Yen Futures price ($/100 yen)	0.7500	0.7300	0.7100	0.6900
Nikkei Contract Size ($)	175,000	177,500	180,000	182,500
Nikkei Contract Size (yen)	23,333,333	24,315,068	25,352,113	26,449,275
Portfolio Value ($)	7,000,000	6,910,667	6,816,000	6,716,000
Portfolio Value (yen)	933,333,333	946,666,667	960,000,000	973,333,333
Portfolio Beta	1	1	1	1
Theoretical Hedge Ratios				
Nikkei Futures	40.0	38.9	37.9	36.8
Yen Futures	74.7	75.7	76.8	77.9
Actual Hedge Positions				
Nikkei Futures	40	40	40	40
Yen Futures	0	0	0	0
Results (Individual Periods)				
Nikkei Futures	—	100,000	100,000	100,000
Yen Futures	—	0	0	0
Combined Futures	—	100,000	100,000	100,000
Portfolio Change ($)	—	−89,333	−94,667	−100,000
Port. Change – Futures	—	−189,333	−194,667	−200,000
Results (Cumulative)				
Nikkei futures	—	100,000	200,000	300,000
Yen Futures	—	0	0	0
Combined Futures	—	100,000	200,000	300,000
Portfolio Change ($)	—	−89,333	−184,000	−284,000
Port. Change – Futures	—	−189,333	−384,000	−584,000

In this example, which is simplified to ignore the potential of basis risk (i.e., values for both Nikkei futures and yen futures are set equal to their respective underlying cash market prices), the initial Nikkei futures position of 40 long contracts is established and maintained without adjustment, but no coincident currency futures participation is incorporated. Given the declining value of the yen over that period, the synthetic position (i.e., the long Nikkei futures without currency exposure) clearly outperforms the maintenance of a traditional Japanese shares portfolio. Ultimately, over the three periods shown, the synthetic exposure generates a profit of $300,000 while the traditional portfolio posts a loss of $284,000—or a difference of $584,000.

In some cases, investors may want to increase exposure to Japanese stocks because they like the Japanese stock market and they expect yen to strengthen, as well. If this were so, then an extra step would be required. That is, the investor would want to add exposure to the yen in addition to the bullish Nikkei futures or options trade. For example, again assume that the Nikkei Index were 35,000, making the dollar value $175,000 (35,000 × $5); and again suppose an investor wanted to commit $7 million to Japanese equities. Assuming yen futures were traded at $0.7500 (per one hundred yen), this exposure would then translate to a ¥933.33 million. Given 12.5 million yen per yen futures contract, to achieve the desired participation would require buying about 75 yen futures contracts. In a similar fashion as that described previously, the trader might alternatively choose to buy calls or sell puts, again with analogous possible outcomes.

Unfortunately, this initial position of currency exposure probably will have to be adjusted as conditions change. For example, if the Nikkei Stock Average were to rally, the original trade would not cover the revised (higher) yen value of the portfolio, and thus additional yen futures (or long calls or short puts) would have to be traded. A declining Nikkei Average would foster the opposite adjustment. Table 21-2 presents an example relating to the former case.

Note that this example also demonstrates a situation where the size of the Nikkei futures (or options) position is also sensitive to exchange rate levels.[2] Importantly, the manner in which this exposure is handled is another business judgment. For example, one might choose to hedge completely, making the dynamic adjustment to both the currency and Nikkei positions as suggested above; or one could hedge portions of the exposure and thereby be somewhat less concerned about the adjustment process. No single approach is necessarily best—or at least one can't be certain in advance of a market move as to which way is best.

Decreasing Exposure to Japanese Equities

The second major application of the Nikkei futures and options is a mechanism to *decrease* the exposure to Japanese equity markets, or to hedge a portfolio of Japanese stocks. As above, the judgment would have to be made as to whether or not one wanted to eliminate exposure to both the currency and the equity portions of the Japanese market, or just one or the other. If one's concern were the currency portion alone, one could maintain the portfolio but hedge the currency. In this case, the hedge instruments could be short yen futures, long put options on yen futures, or short call options. As before, the same problem exists: the quantity of yen requiring coverage is a moving target as the Nikkei Stock Average varies; and thus the currency hedge would likely require some ongoing adjustments as conditions change.

If the currency exposure were acceptable but a reduction in the pure equity exposure were desired, then the use of the Nikkei derivatives, alone, would suffice. In such a case the proper

Table 21–2:
Dynamic Synthetic Equity Exposure

	T0	T1	T2	T3
Nikkei Price Index	35,000	35,500	36,000	36,500
Nikkei Futures Price	35,000	35,500	36,000	36,500
Spot yen prices ($/100 yen)	0.7500	0.7300	0.7100	0.6900
Yen Futures price ($/100 yen)	0.7500	0.7300	0.7100	0.6900
Nikkei Contract Size ($)	175,000	177,500	180,000	182,500
Nikkei Contract Size (yen)	23,333,333	24,315,068	25,352,113	26,449,275
Portfolio Value ($)	7,000,000	6,910,667	6,816,000	6,716,000
Portfolio Value (yen)	933,333,333	946,666,667	960,000,000	973,333,333
Portfolio Beta	1	1	1	1
Theoretical Hedge Ratios				
Nikkei Futures	40.0	38.9	37.9	36.8
Yen Futures	74.7	75.7	76.8	77.9
Actual Hedge Positions				
Nikkei Futures	40	39	38	37
Yen Futures	75	76	77	78
Results (Individual Periods)				
Nikkei Futures	—	100,000	97,500	95,000
Yen Futures	—	–187,500	–190,000	192,500
Combined Futures	—	–87,500	–92,500	–97,500
Portfolio Change ($)	—	–89,333	–94,667	–100,000
Port. Change – Futures	—	–1,833	–2,167	–2,500
Results (Cumulative)				
Nikkei futures	—	100,000	197,500	292,500
Yen Futures	—	–187,500	–377,500	–570,00
Combined Futures	—	–87,500	–180,000	–277,500
Portfolio Change ($)	—	–89,333	–184,000	–284,000
Port. Change – Futures	—	–1,833	–4,000	–6,500

futures hedge ratio calculation would be found identical to that shown in the prior section, though in this case the trader would initiate a short, rather than long, position.

As before, whether to hedge with short futures, short calls or long puts would depend on the desired profit/loss prospects of the particular trader/investor. Perhaps the most general scenario would be one in which the manager wanted to eliminate both currency *and* equity exposures. The hedger would again dissect the problem into the respective pieces and apply both the currency hedge and the CME Nikkei hedge, simultaneously. In this case, the obvious alternative to hedging would be to sell Japanese shares outright; however, the derivative markets would likely be more economical to use than the traditional shares market—particularly if the reduced exposure were expected to be appropriate only for a temporary period. Table 21-3 demonstrates this outcome under a market scenario of a declining Nikkei Average and a weakening yen. The result of this dynamic process is that the combined hedge closely matches the change in the portfolio's dollar value.

Spreading Nikkei vs. S&P 500 Futures

One especially natural trading activity is spreading the Nikkei futures against S&P 500 futures. You would purchase the Index that you expected to perform better, and sell the other. Achieving the objective of this trade, however, requires establishing the positions in the correct proportions, which would be the case when the dollar values of the two respective sides of the spread ("legs") are roughly equivalent.

As an example, suppose you saw the Nikkei futures trading at 33,000 and the S&P 500 futures at 365.00; and suppose further that you expected the Nikkei to out perform the S&P. Constructing the appropriate trade would then involve two steps:

Table 21–3:
Dynamic Short Hedge Example

	T0	T1	T2	T3
Nikkei Price Index	35,000	34,500	34,000	33,500
Nikkei Futures Price	35,000	34,500	34,000	33,500
Spot yen prices ($/100 yen)	0.7500	0.7300	0.7100	0.6900
Yen Futures price ($/100 yen)	0.7500	0.7300	0.7100	0.6900
Nikkei Contract Size ($)	175,000	172,500	170,000	167,500
Nikkei Contract Size (yen)	23,333,333	23,630,137	23,943,662	24,275,362
Portfolio Value ($)	7,000,000	6,716,000	6,437,333	6,164,000
Portfolio Value (yen)	933,333,333	920,000,000	906,666,667	893,333,333
Portfolio Beta	1	1	1	1
Theoretical Hedge Ratios				
Nikkei Futures	–40.0	–38.9	–37.9	–36.8
Yen Futures	–74.7	–73.6	–72.5	–71.5
Actual Hedge Positions				
Nikkei Futures	–40	–39	–38	–37
Yen Futures	–75	–74	–73	–72
Results (Individual Periods)				
Nikkei Futures	—	100,000	97,500	95,000
Yen Futures	—	187,500	185000	182,500
Combined Futures	—	287,500	282,500	277,500
Portfolio Change ($)	—	–284,000	–278,667	–273,333
Port. Change + Futures	—	3,500	3,833	4,167
Results (Cumulative)				
Nikkei futures	—	100,000	197,500	292,500
Yen Futures	—	187,500	372,500	555,00
Combined Futures	—	287,500	570,000	847,500
Portfolio Change ($)	—	–284,000	–562,667	–836,000
Port. Change + Futures	—	3,500	7,333	11,500

Note: Dollar and yen values shown in thousands.

Step 1

Calculate the dollar values of the two respective futures contracts:

Nikkei = 33,000 × $5 = $165,000
S&P 500 = 365.00 × $500 = $182,500

Step 2

Determine the proportion of Nikkei futures to S&P 500 futures by taking the inverse ratio of the two dollar values:

$$\frac{\#\,\text{Nikkei futures}}{\#\,\text{S\&P 500 futures}} \approx \frac{182,500}{165,000} \approx 1.1$$

In this case, a properly balanced hedge would require buying 11 Nikkei futures and selling 10 S&P 500 futures.

One additional caveat is worth noting with regard to these cross index spreads. That is, the futures prices may reflect a "basis bias" that may or may not be desirable. As an example, suppose that when the trade is considered, the Nikkei Average is 32,340 and the S&P 500 is 361.35. Under these conditions, the resulting ratio of the Nikkei Average to the S&P 500 Index is 89.50. The analogous ratio calculated using the given futures prices, however, is 90.41(from 33,000/365.00). Thus, the futures ratio is slightly higher than the index ratio; and, as a result, the forces of "convergence" would tend to push the futures ratio lower, all else remaining constant. For this reason, the basis would be considered to be adverse to the long Nikkei futures/short S&P futures trade (and beneficial to the short Nikkei futures/long S&P futures trade). It should be realized that if the spot ratio had been above the futures ratio, the basis bias would have been reversed.

This chapter is reprinted from *Nikkei Stock Average Futures and Options*, a CME publication, 1991.

Endnotes

1   A second way to achieve an analogous exposure would be
to purchase Japanese stocks via American Depository Receipts (ADRs). ADRs are dollar-denominated securities reg-
istered with the Securities Exchange Commission that trade
outside of Japan. Their prices reflect the share prices of the
stocks upon which the ADRs are based, as well as currency
exchange rates. Thus, ADRs, too, will decline in value with a
weakening yen—the same problem as traditional Japanese
shares.

2   This variability of the correct Nikkei futures hedge ratio
would also occur whenever one wanted to hedge a portfolio
with a given yen valuation. A change in the dollar/yen exchange rate would alter on the dollar value of this portfolio
and thus the number of Nikkei contracts needed to cover it,
even if the level of the Nikkei Stock Average remained un-
changed. For example, with an exchange of $.7500 (per 100
yen), a portfolio of ¥1 billion, and the Nikkei Stock Average
trading at 35,000, approximately 43 Nikkei futures would be
the correct position, from

$$\left(\frac{¥1 \text{ billion} \times \$.0075/¥}{35,000 \times \$5} \right) \approx 43.$$

At an exchange rate of $.8000, three additional long futures
contracts would be required. Analogously, a weakening yen
would necessitate the opposite adjustment.

Index

About the Publisher

PROBUS PUBLISHING COMPANY

Probus Publishing Company fills the informational needs of today's business professional by publishing authoritative, quality books on timely and relevant topics, including:

- Investing
- Futures/Options Trading
- Banking
- Finance
- Marketing and Sales
- Manufacturing and Project Management
- Personal Finance, Real Estate, Insurance and Estate Planning
- Entrepreneurship
- Management

Probus books are available at quantity discounts when purchased for business, educational or sales promotional use. For more information, please call the Director, Corporate/Institutional Sales at 1-800-PROBUS-1, or write:

Director, Corporate/Institutional Sales
Probus Publishing Company
1925 N. Clybourn Avenue
Chicago, Illinois 60614
FAX (312) 868-6250